30-DAY GMAT SUCCESS

by Meng-huan Brandon Wu

Published in the United States by Meng-huan Brandon Wu

www.30daygmatsuccess.com

ISBN: 978-0-615-32627-6

Printed in the United States of America

Table of Contents

1

My 30-Day GMAT Story

Why do you want to go to business school? Why are you studying for the GMAT? Having a clear answer to these questions will help keep you motivated throughout the test preparation and the entire application process, down to the last interviews. Clear answers will also keep your heart pumping during the tough years to come in business school.

I had a hard time deciding on a major in college. Because I was a big fan of video games since I was a kid, I started college majoring in Computer Science, in the hopes of getting a job at a video game company as a software engineer. However, after two years of studying advanced mathematics and programming, I decided that the major was not for me. I was more interested in people, culture, and social interactions than in math and coding. During my junior year, I took various courses ranging from geography to film to try to figure out what was right for me. Finally, I decided on economics and really enjoyed all of my economics classes throughout college.

After college, I started my professional life as a financial consultant in a foreign currency exchange company. Little did I know that the company was a disaster, as it lost two-thirds of my client's money within a month. I left soon after learning more about the company's shady practices, and decided to give video games another try. I join Electronic Arts, the largest video game publisher at the time, as a tester. I was paid a lowly $10 an hour, or not much more than what you get paid to work at a McDonald's. Soon after I joined the company, I was promoted to lead a small team of testers and worked on a product that eventually became one of the most popular PC games of all time. I worked on a couple more projects before I decided that it was time to accelerate my career by pursuing a graduate degree. Although I really enjoyed my job, my low salary was putting pressure on me. I applied for a master's program in computer science at Carnegie Mellon University and learned in December 2004 that I had been accepted.

In January 2005, I took a vacation and spent a month in my hometown visiting family and old friends before school started. Many of my friends asked me what I planned to do next, and I told them that I would be starting a master's program in computer science. However, after answering that question a couple of times, I began to lose faith in my answer. Hadn't I switched my major in college from computer science? Was computer science really the right choice for me? All of these thoughts came back to me and I ended up spending the majority of my vacation pondering my future. One day, as I was walking through the financial district, I realized that an infinite number of possibilities existed in the world of business. Why limit myself to video games and software? I started looking into business schools and decided that, instead of going to Carnegie Mellon, I would try to get into a business school.

It was February when I decided to apply to business schools, and the deadline for the last rounds of applications was early March. I had exactly one month to prepare the application, get recommendation letters, finish all of the essays, and take the GMAT. The earliest deadline for the schools to which I was applying was March 5th, so I registered to take the GMAT on exactly one day before the deadline, on March 4th.

Early morning on test day, with my notebook in a small shoulder bag, I headed out to the test center in downtown San Francisco. I arrived 30 minutes before the start time, so sat in front of the building to review my notebook. I remember seeing businessmen walking on the street, street vendors selling pretzels and hotdogs, and a couple of tourists trying to find their way to Union Square. What a fine day, I thought, and I had to take this test instead of enjoy the beautiful sunshine!

The computers in the test centers were old, and the monitors flickered at my eyes during the entire test. When I finished the test, I saw the score on the screen and couldn't believe my eyes! 780?! I was hoping for above 700, but never expected to get 780! I was on my way out of the test center when the administrator congratulated me. "Wow, you did really well!" she said. I was still in shocked and replied, "Oh, nah I did just OK…" Hah, I still remember the confused look on her face after I said that ☺.

A couple of months later, I entered one of the top schools of my choice with a tuition grant. My work experience was much shorter than the average, but my high GMAT score helped my application. The hard work that I had put in during the month that I had prepared for the GMAT had definitely paid off!

Where Am I Now?

Fast-forward three years. I now work in Tokyo at the headquarters strategy office of one of the largest consumer electronics companies in the world. My salary is four times what I had been earning prior to business school, and I truly enjoy the challenging and rewarding nature of my job. The best part is that I know that with an MBA degree and the knowledge and skills that I gained in business school, my career options are limitless. Getting an MBA was one of the best investments that I made in myself, and you can also experience this!

2

INTRODUCTION: THE GMAT

Congratulations! You have decided to take the time to learn how to master one of the most important tests that you will ever face in your life, the GMAT. The Graduate Management Admissions Test (GMAT) is designed to measure how successful one will be in business school. Business schools use the results of the GMAT, along with recommendation letters, essays, and other application materials, when making decisions on admitting applicants to their MBA programs.

The test is administered on a computer in North America. In some areas of the world outside of North America, it is a paper-based test given at test centers. The fee to take the test is $250 regardless of where you are taking it. You can schedule a GMAT online at http://www.mba.com/.

The GMAT evaluates the verbal, math, and writing skills that you have developed through your educational and professional experiences. The GMAT does not measure your business knowledge or professional skills, nor does it measure other skills such as creativity, motivation, and interpersonal skills. The GMAT is designed to allow a person who does not have English as his or her first language to still perform well. That said, it may not always reflect accurately the abilities of a person whose first language is not English.

Registration

You can register online at MBA.com and pay your registration fee by credit card, or you may call one of the following numbers to schedule an appointment at a test center:

Americas

Telephone (toll-free within the U.S. & Canada only): 1-800-717-GMAT (4628)

Telephone: 1-952-681-3680

Victoria, British Columbia

Telephone: 1-866-442-GMAT (4628)

Asia Pacific

Telephone: +603 8318-9961

India

Telephone: +91 (0) 120 439 7830

Europe/Middle East/Africa

Telephone: +44 (0) 161 855 7219

To apply via mail or fax, or to register as a test taker with disabilities, please follow the instructions provided at http://www.mba.com/mba/thegmat/scheduleagmatappointment.

Try to schedule your appointment weeks in advance to ensure that you get a spot.

GMAT scores are valid at most institutions in the country for up to five years from the date that you took the exam.

Test Structure

The GMAT is divided into three sections: the Analytical Writing Assessment, the Quantitative Section, and the Verbal Section.

The exam starts with the **Analytical Writing Assessment (AWA)**. You need to write two different types of articles, an Analysis of an Issue and an Analysis of an Argument. You have 30 minutes to write each article.

The **Quantitative Section** starts after an optional ten-minute break and contains 37 multiple-choice questions. You have 75 minutes to complete this section. The questions are categorized into two groups: Problem Solving and Data Sufficiency. We will talk about both types of questions in more detail.

The **Verbal Section** starts after another optional ten-minute break, and contains 41 multiple-choice questions. You have 75 minutes to complete this section. The questions are categorized into three groups: Reading Comprehension, Critical Reasoning, and Sentence Correction. We'll also talk about these questions in detail.

Analytical Writing Assessment

This section consists of two essays, an Analysis of an Issue and an Analysis of an Argument. You have 30 minutes to finish each essay, and you are marked on a scale from 0 to 6. Two readers read an essay and grade it in half-point (0.5) increments. If the two scores from the readers are within one point of each other, then the average of the two is used. If a more than one-point difference exists, then a third reader grades the essay.

Now, when we talk about readers, we are not talking just about humans. The first reader is Intellimetric, a computer program that analyzes your writing and syntax abilities. The second and, if needed, third readers are humans who evaluate the quality of your ideas, your organizational ability, and how you develop and express your ideas.

The evaluators understand that English is not always the first language for test takers, and minor errors and mistakes are often expected. There is no need to worry about your essay being grammatically perfect. You will also find that most of the business schools that you apply to do not care much about this portion of the test. For them, the verbal and quantitative sections are the most important. Therefore, focus the majority of your preparation time on these two sections.

Quantitative Section

This section contains 37 multiple-choice questions and you have 75 minutes to complete the entire section. You will find two types of questions: Problem Solving and Data Sufficiency. You can score between 0 and 60 points on this section.

Problem Solving

This type of question measures your quantitative reasoning ability (arithmetic, algebra, and geometry) by presenting a series of multiple-choice problems in either plain math format form or more complex word / sentence form. Sometimes, the questions use diagrams, but be careful as they are not always drawn to scale.

Data Sufficiency

Data Sufficiency questions test your ability to analyze and identify the information required to solve a quantitative problem. It starts with a question and two statements that contain information related to the question. You have to decide whether the two statements are sufficient to solve the question. The answers to this type of question are always presented as follows.

- Statement (1) ALONE is sufficient, but statement (2) is not sufficient.
- Statement (2) ALONE is sufficient, but statement (1) is not sufficient.
- BOTH statements TOGETHER are sufficient, but NEITHER statement ALONE is sufficient.
- EACH statement ALONE is sufficient.
- Statements (1) and (2) TOGETHER are NOT sufficient.

Verbal Section

The verbal section contains 41 multiple-choice questions and you have 75 minutes to complete this section. You will find three types of questions: Reading Comprehension, Critical Reasoning, and Sentence Correction. You can score between 0 and 60 points in this section.

Sentence Correction

This part of the test focuses on correct expression (grammar and structure) and effective expression (clarity and concision), and evaluates your grammar and logic skills, and ability to craft an effective sentence. The questions consist of a sentence and five associated answers. You choose the best way to restructure the sentence to express the same meaning, and you want to choose the answer that creates the clearest and most exact sentence without changing its meaning.

Critical Reasoning

Critical Reasoning questions test your reasoning skills. Understanding the logic behind the assumptions and conclusions is crucial for these questions, as is your skill in evaluating the strengths and weakness of the argument. For some of the questions, you may find that more than one answer is correct, and you need to select the "best" answer out of all of the "correct" answers.

Reading Comprehension

This section tests your ability to read critically and answer questions related to the passages presented. The passages are on a range of topics, from sociology and sciences, to business. The questions test how well you understand the passage and the information presented. No specific knowledge about the topics is required to answer the questions.

Typically, passages in this section are up to 350 words, with three or more questions based on their content. This section evaluates your ability to:

- Understand expressions, statements, and sometimes quantitative concepts in the passages;
- Understand the logic and arguments presented in the passages; and

- Infer facts and statements based on the information contained in the passages.

Your Score

Now we come to what really matters: your score. Your GMAT score is calculated from the quantitative and verbal sections, and does not include the Analytical Writing Assessment section. Your score will fall between 200 and 800.

Questions are dynamically selected as you take the test. The GMAT is called a computer-adaptive test, as it uses your answers to questions to determine the next questions to present to you, allowing you to obtain a score that reflects the level of difficulty of the questions that you answer correctly. If you answer a question correctly, the next question will be harder. If you answer a question incorrectly, the next question will be easier. The strategy here is to spend a little more time on the earlier questions so that the system places you at a higher rank, and continues to give you harder questions. This will, in the end, give you a better chance of getting higher scores.

REMEMBER TO SPEND MORE TIME ON THE EARLIER QUESTIONS!

An important thing to remember that cannot be stressed enough is: **LEAVING A QUESTION BLANK WILL HURT YOUR SCORE MORE THAN IF YOU ANSWER A QUESTION INCORRECTLY!**

This is very important to remember. The GMAT is not like the SAT, which has a penalty for answering questions incorrectly. Always guess if you don't know the answer to a question, or if you are pressed for time.

Retaking the Test

If you need to retake the GMAT, you may do so once every 31 calendar days and no more than five times within a 12-month period.

3

STUDY SCHEDULE

Now that we have established a basic understanding of the structure of the GMAT, let's take a look at how we will efficiently use the time you have to study over the next 30 days. The goal of this study schedule is to help you plan your preparation to make the best use of your limited time. I will keep everything simple, short, and easy to digest. Information overflow is never efficient or effective, and reading a lot of words doesn't mean that you are absorbing what you need to know.

What Else You Need

1. **Official GMAT Guide.** Try to practice only with official questions. Although questions from other sources may be good, using the official questions will:
    - Help you understand exactly what to expect on test day;
    - Help you focus on real questions from past exams by reducing information overflow.

You won't find many practice questions in this book. I see little value in trying to emulate these questions or to create "GMAT-style" questions here when you can get authentic questions directly from the source that creates the actual GMAT questions. Instead, we will focus on planning your study schedule and on what you need to learn. I recommend three official GMAT books. You should get the first one. Then, decide whether you need more practice and get the other two.

- The Official Guide for GMAT Review
- The Official Guide for GMAT Verbal Review
- The Official Guide for GMAT Quantitative Review

2. **A notebook, preferably one with a calendar.** This is one of the most important tools that you will use throughout your preparation. Find a notebook that is easy for you to write in and easy to carry around, as it will be central to your studying. Make sure to get a notebook that you like because you will spend the entire month with it. It will also be the most important test preparation material that you bring to the test center on test day. I recommend that you find a larger notebook so that you can write clearly; a larger notebook will also be easier to read.

3. **A stop timer.** This serves two purposes:

    - Measures your test taking time;
    - Keeps you on schedule with your study plan and makes sure that you are putting in enough hours both studying and getting rest.

4. **Relaxation tools.** Video games, TV/DVD/Blu-ray, hot baths, etc. Anything that can help you relax within 30 to 60 minutes. You will need some kind of entertainment tool to help you relax during this one month. Non-stop studying without taking a break will result in diminishing returns on your efforts. Get yourself a relaxation tool as a reward for completing sections of your preparation.

5. **Determination.** Determination. Determination! The GMAT is not easy, and even if you have all of the help that the world has to offer, you still need to put in the hours studying for it. Starting today for one month, all of the books that you read should be related to the GMAT, and the only information that you absorb into your head should be related to the GMAT. Give up your social life for the next four weekends, turn off your cell phone, and forget about watching TV everyday. This will be one of the toughest months of your life. You will live and breathe the GMAT. You will get tired and feel stressed. But when you come out of the test center one month later, you will thank yourself for making these sacrifices. Committing yourself to prepare for the GMAT this month will be one of the best investments that you make in yourself. A high GMAT score opened a wealth of opportunities for me, both in terms of career and self-growth. And it can do the same for you!

Everyone is different and so should his or her study plans be. To customize a study plan for you, I have structured the book into several parts. You will jump back and forth among chapters and study according to the study plan we create together. DO NOT READ THIS BOOK FROM THE FIRST PAGE TO THE LAST! Follow the instructions and study accordingly.

Phase I Study Schedule

There are three phases in our study plan. Schedule for the first 10 days:

Day 1	Day 2	Day 3	Day 4	Day 5
1st test, Setting priorities	Scheduling, Test review	Group 4, Practice Test, Review	Group 4	Group 3
Day 6	**Day 7**	**Day 8**	**Day 9**	**Day 10**
Group 2	Group 1, Rest	Group 4	Group 3	Group 2 and 1

DAY I:

My first mistake when preparing for the GMAT was not knowing what to study! Like most people, on the first day of my journey to taking the GMAT, I opened a GMAT study guide and started reading. At the end of that day, I felt clueless and lost, and had no idea what I had just learned and what I should study the next day. To avoid confusion and wasting time, let's first define our direction before starting our journey.

Before you do any studying, take a practice test today. The goal here is not to get a high score – great if you do, but that's not the point. The goal here is to find out your weaknesses. Everyone has different strengths and weaknesses. You may already be good at parts of the test and need more time preparing for other parts. Today, the goal is to identify what you find most difficult and plan your study accordingly. This will maximize your study return on investment (ROI). Don't worry about not knowing anything about the GMAT yet. The more problems and difficulties that we can identify today, the better. So get out your stop timer and Official GMAT Guide, set aside 75 minutes for the verbal section and 75 minutes for the math section, turn off your cell phone, and find a place where you will not be interrupted.

Come back to this section after you take the test and before you check your answers. We want to discuss your test-taking experience before you check your answers.

Go ahead and take the practice exam now. And remember to time yourself with your stop timer.

------ take the full test ----- 2.5 hr

or

------ take either the full verbal or math test ----- 1hr and 15 min

and take the other test on day 2

----- return here after the test -----

Congratulations, you have just finished your first GMAT experience. Don't check your answers yet. We will do that in a bit. First, let's discuss your test-taking experience.

Take out your notebook and write down the first answer that comes to mind to the following questions (don't think too hard on these):

1. Which did you find harder, the math section or the verbal section?

   Ex. VERBAL

2. From your answer above, what part of that section was the most difficult? Rank the parts of the section in order of difficulty level (most difficult to least difficult).

   Ex. Sentence Correction => Critical Reasoning => Reading Comprehension

3. From the other section of the test, rank its parts in terms of difficulty.

   Ex. Data Sufficiency => Problem Solving

4. How much of the test were you able to complete within the time limit (answer in a percentage)?

   Ex. About 50% completed.

5. Write down any other issues that you noticed while taking the test.

   Ex. My eyes got really dry after the first hour. Maybe it's my contact lenses.

Now, check your answers against the correct answers for the test. Rank the sections according to how well you did percentage-wise, and write this in your notebook. For example:

(SC) Sentence Correction: 70% correct

(CR) Critical Reasoning: 60% correct

(RC) Reading Comprehension; 80% correct

(PS) Problem Solving: 85% correct

(DS) Data Sufficiency: 80% correct

Ranking: CR => SC => DS/RC => PS

Now let's prioritize your study plan. Look at the ranking before and after you checked your answers. Let's compare your comfort level with each section versus your performance on each section.

Divide the sections into four groups:

1. Comfortable, good performance (Group 1)

   You have a good grasp of the material being tested, and feel confident when being tested on these sections. Let's not worry so much about these sections right now.

2. Uncomfortable, good performance (Group 2)

   You might feel nervous about these sections, probably because you are not familiar with the test or the format/style of these sections. But with the existing knowledge that you have, you can do quite well. We will focus on familiarizing you with the formats and styles of these sections, and will not worry so much about knowledge related to these sections.

3. Comfortable, poor performance (Group 3)

   You are confident about these sections, maybe because you had prior experience with a similar topic. But you have obviously forgotten some of the material that you need to know to ace these sections. We will need to focus on getting your knowledge back in place for these sections.

4. Uncomfortable, poor performance (Group 4)

   These sections are your top priority. You are not familiar with the form of the sections, and you need a lot of work on learning the knowledge related to these sections. These sections are a TOP PRIORITY!

Each section should belong to one of these groups. And, each group should have at least one section assigned to it (one of the groups will contain two sections). We will focus your study from Group 4 back to Group 1. Mark your findings in your notebook.

I made a big mistake while I was studying. I was so overly confident with the math sections, specifically the problem-solving section, that I completely ignored them until three days before the exam. I was caught off guard during the exam and got stuck on a few problem-solving questions, costing me precious exam time and resulting in a lower math score than my verbal score. Despite my high comfort level with math, I did better on the verbal section than on the math section. This is why I asked you to rank the sections twice, once according to your comfort level and once according to your performance. Considering both when prioritizing your study is crucial to creating a winning study strategy.

Good job today. You have finished your first day of GMAT studying. Not so difficult, is it? Get good rest tonight, as we will dive into the materials tomorrow with the blueprint that you have just created.

DAY 2

Ready for the second day of your GMAT journey? Yesterday we established your priorities for studying for the GMAT based on the group system that we developed. Remember the last two questions that you answered right after your took the test?

- How much of the test were you able to complete within the time limit ? (state in a percentage)
- Write down any other issues that you noticed during the test.

If you weren't able to complete the test in time and answered less than 30% of the questions, let's indicate "time" in Group 4 as a priority. If you noticed any other issues during the test that might have a major impact on your score, keep them in mind (and in your notebook). We need to deal with these issues before test day.

Our next step is to plan our study schedule. Since we only have 29 days left, we need to plan accordingly to ensure that we use our time efficiently. Remember, the goal is not to absorb the greatest amount of information, but rather to absorb the information most relevant for you.

Macro Schedule

We will divide our study into three major phases. In Phase I, we will familiarize ourselves with the logic of the GMAT to basically learn how writers of the test think. The GMAT does not test your knowledge of the world; it is, as is any other standardized test, a test of how well you understand the test itself. We need to abandon our own thinking at times and adapt to the "GMAT way of thinking." We will spend 10 days on this phase to train our brain for this purpose. And we do this by spending the majority of the time studying individual questions and answers in an attempt to understand why the answers are considered "GMAT correct."

In Phase II, we will dive into various techniques and tips for taking the test. There are millions of test-taking techniques, and learning all of them simply isn't possible given the amount of time that we have. Instead, I will tell you about the techniques that worked for me when I took the test. Some of them are simple, and some may seem trivial and obvious. But keep in mind that we are not trying to become scholars. We want effectiveness, and the best techniques for you are the ones that are simple to implement and, at the same time, give you the greatest improvement on your scores. We will spend 10 days during this period learning and mastering these techniques.

In Phase III, we will do only two things:

1. Review what you learned;
2. Get ready for the test day.

It is useless to continue learning new techniques when you are near the test day. The pressure will be too great for you to absorb any new information. Instead, we will make sure that we remember everything that we have learned, and ensure that we are physically and mentally ready for the test.

As we progress, you will gradually spend less time on the planning part of the book and more on the skill-building part that follows this section.

Micro Schedule

Having a fixed daily study schedule will force you to study. It will also get your body accustomed to following fixed schedules—something you will need to do on test day.

Phase I Study Cycle

Our goal in Phase I is to familiarize you with the test. Therefore, you will spend three to four hours each day on one "cycle" that focuses on the test and the test review. One cycle consists of three sessions and is defined as follows:

10% – Test Preparation + Review Previous Test

50% – Practice Test

40% – Test Review

If you can spend four hours a day studying, your cycle will be broken down roughly as follows:

30 minutes – Test Preparation + Test Review (previous test)

120 minutes – Practice Test

90 minutes – Test Review

If you spend three hours a day, your cycle will be broken down roughly as follows:

20 minutes – Test Preparation + Test Review (previous test)

90 minutes – Practice Test

70 minutes – Test Review

Session Definitions

Test Preparation – Study GMAT prep materials and review previously studied materials. Review the mistakes that you made on the previous day if you weren't able to finish the test. Participate in online forums to learn about the common mistakes that people make, and the questions that most people find difficult to answer. In Phase I, as we familiarize ourselves with the test, spend most of your time reviewing explanations for answers from the Official Guide and less time on the techniques. In Phase II, start to shift your focus to the various test-taking techniques. If you have time, participate in online forums starting in Phase II.

Practice Test – Take one full practice test, or do the practice questions for the sections you are studying that day. Time yourself during the practice test, and circle all of the questions that you find difficult. If you are unsure about the answer to a particular question but were able to narrow your answer down to two or three choices, circle that question as well.

Test Review – Check your answers against the correct answers provided by the book. Circle the ones that you answered incorrectly. After checking the answers, review all of the questions you marked as difficult, and all of the questions that you answered incorrectly. Carefully review each one of them and write down in your notebook anything that you learned. Keep in mind that the goal is not to write down a lot of information; just note the most important principles and key findings. In Phase I, we will spend some time in the beginning of the cycle each day to review the test you took on the previous day if you weren't able to finish reviewing it.

I studied four hours a day when I was preparing for the GMAT, and I strongly recommend that you try to study for at least four hours a day. Of course, this depends on how busy you are with your current job and other commitments. But try to spend at least three hours a day studying. Decide on how much time each day you can spend studying and set aside a fixed period during the day for this. You should be studying roughly at the same time each day to help you stay focused and on schedule with your study plan. Use your stop timer to make sure that you put in the amount of time that you have committed to.

On the weekends, you should do two cycles each day. You only have four weekends before the test so let's not waste them.

I kept myself to this schedule for a month, non-stop. It was very difficult at first. There were so many other things that I would rather have been doing, and forcing myself to stay focused wasn't easy. But after the first week, it became easier and easier. I was able to train myself to focus on the test and the prep materials. Persistence will be your key to success, so commit to this schedule and do the best that you can. Remember, you are doing this for yourself, and you will thank yourself very soon for being committed.

Remember the study blueprint that you designed yesterday? We will spend the rest of today reviewing the sections in Group 4 – the sections that are uncomfortable and difficult for you. If you have more than one section in Group 4, select only one section for today. Review the selected section carefully from the practice test you took yesterday. For each question that you answered incorrectly, study the explanations in the Official Guide and spend as much time as it takes for you to understand "why" the answer you picked wasn't correct, and why the "correct" answer is correct. Read the explanation multiple times and try to familiarize yourself with how the authors of the Official Guide think. Even if the explanation doesn't make sense to you, try not to argue with it; rather, rationalize that answer and get used to the logic presented in the Official Guide. Use your notebook and write down things that you find new or particularly difficult, especially idioms or commonly tested phrases. Don't worry if you can't find many of them, this is only your first test.

Many people argue that the explanations in the Official Guide are no good and that other test-taking methods are more effective. I don't disagree with studying other test-taking methods, but I have found that the combination of studying the "official logic" and "test-taking secrets" helped me to quickly achieve a high GMAT score.

The key for today is to start to understand the logic behind GMAT questions. There is no better way to do this than studying the explanations in the Official Guide. You will have a very difficult time understanding them right now, because you are just getting started and because the logic behind GMAT questions isn't always obvious. But with the time that you spend studying for the GMAT, you will become familiar with them quickly and be able to easily spot the correct answer choices.

After reviewing your priority section(s), review the rest of the sections quickly using the same approach but spend less time on them if you get stuck. I suggest that you do not use up too much of your energy today. We have a long battle ahead of us.

DAY 3

Let's continue working on our goal for Phase I – to learn the logics of the GMAT. Yesterday, if you weren't able to finish reviewing a section from Group 4, review it now and come back when you are finished.

Today will be the first day of your "regular" day in which you exercise one study cycle. In the next couple of days, you will follow roughly the same study schedule. You will also spend much less time on this part of the book and more on the practice test and the study materials.

Let's now jump to the study material sections of this book. We will start with your priority 1 section based on the priorities that you set on the first day. This section should also be the same one you reviewed yesterday. Remember not to read for more than 25% of the time allocated for studying today because we still have to take our practice test and do the test review. The goal is not to read a lot, but to memorize a few points that can be useful for you. Make sure that you understand what you read. Reread anything that you find confusing, and don't skim through the materials. Again, write down in your notebook what you find difficult or hard to remember. Return here after studying.

OK, let's take a short five- to ten-minute break before we start the practice test. Drink some water and make sure you are well hydrated. Over 70% of our daily fatigue is caused by a lack of adequate water intake. You can also try drinking coffee or tea to see if they will have any effect on you when taking the test. It is better to find out now rather than later.

Depending on the time that you have allocated and your level of knowledge of the GMAT, you can take one full test, only the verbal section, only the math section, or selected parts of the test. We will be more flexible during Phase I of studying, so you don't necessarily need to do full sets now. We will start taking full sets later when we take time management into consideration.

For the practice test today, start with sections from Group 4 and/or Group 3. Spend as much time as you need to on each question, and thoroughly consider your answer. Circle all of the questions that you find difficult. Also circle the answers that you are unsure of. If you think that answers A and C are both good answers for a particular question, circle the question, answer A, and answer C. This will help you determine what to study for and where your weaknesses are during your reviews.

Go ahead and take the test now. Return here and continue reading after you have finished.

It's time for the review. First, check your answers against the correct answers and circle the questions that you answered incorrectly. Don't read the explanations until you've finished checking all of your answers.

Now, review all of the questions and answers that you circled today. These include questions that you found difficult to answer during the test, and questions that you answered incorrectly. Review each one carefully, and try to understand the explanations as best as you can using the principles we discussed yesterday. See if you can identify questions that can be solved using techniques that you learned today. Also, don't forget to use your notebook! Write down anything you learned while reviewing the test today.

Again, spend as much time as it takes on your priority sections and really try to understand them. After you've reviewed your priority sections, if you still have some time, quickly review the rest of the test.

Great! You have completed your first study cycle. Give yourself a pat on the back and get ready to do this again tomorrow.

DAY 4

Today we will again focus your on your priority sections from Group 4. If you have more than one section in Group 4, study the other section today. Since you completed one study cycle yesterday, you know the drill. We will do the same exercise today. Remember, spend 10% of your time on Test Preparation, 50% of your time on the Practice Test, and 40% on Test Review. If you weren't able to finish reviewing the test yesterday, review it now before going into the study materials. Again, don't try to read everything today. Instead, spend your time understanding the materials and focusing your energy on just a few things.

After studying the materials, pick sections from Group 4 and/or Group 3 for today's practice test. Spend as much time as you need to on each question, and think thoroughly about your answer. Circle all of the questions that you find difficult during the test. Also circle the answers that you are unsure of.

After the practice test, take a five- to ten-minute break. Now check your answers against the correct answers and circle all of the questions you answered incorrectly. Review all of the questions and answers that you circled today. Again, these should include questions that you found difficult to answer and questions that you answered incorrectly. Review each one carefully and try to understand the explanation. Write down in your notebook anything that you learned while reviewing the test today.

Again, spend as much time as it takes for you to understand the questions and answers. If you have difficulty agreeing with a particular explanation, my advice is to simply accept the explanation and try to adapt to the logic behind it. It might not be the most logical answer to you, but it is the most logical answer according to the GMAT. That reason alone is enough for us to adapt to this logic. After your priority sections, quickly review the rest of the test.

You have now completed Day 4 of your GMAT journey.

DAY 5

Today we're on the same schedule as yesterday, but will focus on section(s) in Group 3 – the sections you feel comfortable with but do not perform well on. You may have prior experiences with these sections in Group 3, but don't overlook these questions. Some GMAT questions may seem easy, but don't be fooled! They often require much more thinking if you want to answer them correctly. Often, people can improve their scores in Group 3 by learning to be careful. I hope that you also do that today, and practice being patient with questions that appear simple.

Again, spend 10% of your time on Test Preparation, 50% on taking the Practice Test, and 40% on the Test Review.

DAY 6

You are probably pretty familiar with the schedule by now. Today we will focus on Group 2 – the sections of the test where you feel uncomfortable but actually performed well. You most likely know the materials well, but do not have sufficient practice in these areas. Today should be relatively easy for you.

Same drill: Test Prep, Practice Test, and Test Review.

DAY 7

Today should be a piece of cake for you – Group 1. You know the materials well and can achieve good scores in these areas. We just want to make sure that you are spending enough practice time in all areas of the test, so don't overlook today's study schedule.

Remember that I mentioned in the beginning of the book that you need relaxation tools? Today is the day when you can use these tools to reward yourself after a tough week! Watch TV, play video games, or go to a karaoke bar (but try to stay away from alcohol as it might affect your study after today). You studied hard for the past week, and today you should try to relax and recharge. Spend 30 minutes to an hour on these recreational activities after your study cycle today.

DAY 8

Hope you had enough rest yesterday. We are almost done with Phase I – understanding the logic of the GMAT. Hopefully, you are feeling a bit more familiar with GMAT-style questions and, more importantly, the logic behind the correct answers.

We are back on our regular 10–50–40 schedule today – 10% Test Preparation, 50% Practice Test, 40% Test Review. Today, we will go back to Group 4 and tackle the most difficult sections.

DAY 9

Group 3 is the name of the game today. Last time we looked, this was the section where being a little more careful can really improve your performance. Continue with this principle and let's try these sections again today.

And remember, go deep with each question!

DAY 10

Today is the last day of our study Phase I, and we will focus on Group 2 and Group 1 sections – the areas where you performed well. Let's finish your study cycle first and then do a quick review of your first ten days of GMAT preparation. Come back after you finish the study cycle for today.

After today, we will have completed 30% of our GMAT preparation. How do you feel about the test after ten days of studying? You should have a pretty good sense of how the questions are structured and how most answer choices are constructed. Your notebook should also contain quite a few notes that you have written down during the past ten days.

Tomorrow, we will start Phase II of your GMAT preparation. We will focus more on the study materials and various test-taking techniques. If you didn't finish reading the study materials for all of the sections, we will finish them in the next ten days. We will also review other materials to help you prepare for the test.

Before we finish for today, review your notes and circle the points that you still feel unfamiliar with. And then get a good rest tonight!

After ten days of studying, we have established three things.

1. You are now familiar with the test format.
2. You are now familiar with the test logic.
3. You are now familiar with the study schedule.

In the next ten days, we will try to achieve the following three things:

1. Learn the most effective GMAT techniques;
2. Understand your GMAT level (score);
3. Participate in study groups or online forums; however, don't spend too much time on this and watch out for information overflow.

We will first focus our study on various GMAT test-taking techniques. You have already studied some of them in Phase I. In Phase II, we will spend a lot more of our energy on learning and using these techniques to improve your scores.

Also, while I was studying, I found out that having someone else studying alongside with me was a great help. I participated in various GMAT forums in which members helped each other better prepare for the test. Not only can you find difficult questions discussed on these forums, you will also be more motivated knowing that others like you are working hard to prepare for the GMAT. Just like you, most business school candidates are highly motivated individuals, and having these people around you will help you not only with preparing for the GMAT, but with all other aspects of applying to and surviving B-school. You can find popular online GMAT forums by searching for "GMAT FORUM" on search engines such as http://www.google.com or http://www.yahoo.com. Remember, a forum is only as good as its members, so try a few different ones to find a community that fits your study and communication style.

Phase II Study Cycle

You are pretty familiar with our study schedule from Phase I. The study cycle in Phase II is similar – you will just spend slightly less time reviewing tests and a bit more time learning techniques.

In Phase II, one cycle is defined as follows:

25% – Test Preparation

50% – Practice Test

25% – Test Review

If you spend four hours a day to study, your cycle will be:

60 minutes – Test Preparation

120 minutes – Practice Test

60 minutes – Test Review

If you spend three hours a day, your cycle will be:

45 minutes – Test Preparation

90 minutes – Practice Test

45 minutes – Test Review

As you can see, your daily study cycle is now 25–50–25. We have increased the time allocated for Test Preparation to allow time to learn test techniques. You will also spend more time on the skill-building part of this book and less on the planning part. Starting today, you will exercise this study cycle for ten days and will study the following sections/groups:

Day 11	Day 12	Day 13	Day 14	Day 15
Phase II: Group 4	Group 4	Group 3	Group 2,1	Group of your choice, Rest
Day 16	**Day 17**	**Day 18**	**Day 19**	**Day 20**
Start spending less time on individual questions. Group 4	Group 4	Group 3	Group 2,1	Group of your choice, Rest

DAY 11 (GROUP 4)

Today we focus on your Group 4 section(s). Start your test preparation now and head over to the skill-building part of the book to learn and review test-taking techniques for these section(s). Then start taking practice questions for Group 4 section(s). Try to apply the techniques that you learned today. Review the practice test afterwards.

DAY 12 (GROUP 4)

Stick to the same routine as yesterday, again focusing on Group 4. From today, you can start participating in the online forums suggested above after test review, but remember not to spend too much time comparing your performance with other people. Remember to focus on your own study!

DAY 13 (GROUP 3)

Today, we will learn some techniques for Group 3. Again, feel free to participate in the online forums if you have time after your test review. And don't forget to utilize your notebook!

DAY 14 (GROUPS 1 AND 2)

Focus on Groups 2 and 1 today, the sections you are most familiar with. If you find yourself finishing early, spend some time reviewing your notes to see if you are happy with the way you are organizing information.

DAY 15 (GROUP OF YOUR CHOICE, CATCH UP, REST)

On Day 15, you can pick one or two sections that you feel less confident with and study them on this day. Also use this day to catch up on any review or study activities that you might have missed.

Don't forget to give yourself a pat on the shoulder and rest a bit today. Reward yourself and have a little fun today ☺.

Starting on Day 16, we will spend slightly less time on each individual question or answer, and will transition our efforts from understanding the test to efficiently managing our time during the test.. Start timing yourself when taking your practice test and compare that with the allowed time for each section.

Remember you have 75 minutes to answer 41 questions in the verbal section, which equals roughly 1.8 minutes per question (1 minute and 48 seconds). And, you have 75 minutes to answer 37 questions in the math section, or roughly 2 minutes per question.

DAY 16 (GROUP 4)

We are back to Group 4 again for today and tomorrow. You should feel much more comfortable with your Group 4 section(s) after tomorrow given all of the practice that you have had.

DAY 17 (GROUP 4)

No need for further introduction, as you are working on Group 4 again today. Have fun and enjoy! You know that you are conquering this section ☺.

DAY 18 (GROUP 3)

You should feel quite comfortable with Group 3 now. Remember to time yourself against the allowed two minutes per question, if possible.

DAY 19 (GROUPS 1 AND 2)

Focus on Groups 2 and 1 today, the sections you are most familiar with. If you find yourself finishing early again, review your notes and focus on what you've forgotten.

DAY 20 (CHOICE, CATCH UP, REST)

Select a few sections that you want to polish up on today and take your practice questions for those sections. Afterwards, review your notes and all of the questions that you highlighted in the last four days. Remember, your notebook is the textbook that you customized for yourself. Thus, it is the most important tool when it comes to test day. Make sure that you are familiar with every note that you've taken and keep your notebook well organized. Finally, feel free to rest and relax completely today. We are going into the final ten days of your GMAT journey and you want to be physically and mentally ready!

Phase III Study Schedule

Here is your schedule for the final ten days:

Day 21	Day 22	Day 23	Day 24	Day 25
Full-set	Full-set	Full-set	Review	Full-set
Day 26	Day 27	Day 28	Day 29	Day 30
Full-set	Full-set	Review	Review	Review

DAY 21 TO DAY 27 (TIME MANAGEMENT, FULL SET)

Congratulations! You've finished two-thirds of the course and are now well equipped with the techniques required for the GMAT. We have roughly ten days from today to your test day.

In Phase III, your daily study cycle should look like this:

150 minutes – Practice Test (75 minutes verbal, 75 minutes math)

90+ minutes – Test Review

If you don't have the time to do a full set every day, do half a set every day and alternate between the verbal and the math sections.

Do a full set during the Practice Test period, and then check the answers during Test Review. Also during Test Review, review the materials that you've learned. We are putting all of our efforts into getting ready for test day, and doing these full sets will help you get familiar with how the actual test will be. As mentioned before, in Phase III, we will do only two things:

1. Review what you learned;
2. Get ready for test day.

If you couldn't finish some materials from the previous ten days, don't worry. We have some time for you to study them. However, try to finish all of the materials by day 26 or 27 (five to six days from today) if possible, and leave the last few days for just reviewing materials and getting ready for test day.

Let's talk about time management for a moment. Managing your time during the test is one of the most important factors that will affect your score. No matter how prepared you are for the verbal or math sections, poor time management can prevent you from getting your desired score.

Spend no more than four to five minutes on each question early in the test, and no more than two minutes later on in the test for the same section. As discussed, the earlier part of the section will have a greater impact on your final score than the latter part of the same section, so focus and spend more time on the early part. On the other hand, don't think too much about any one question when working on the latter part of the section. You will have less time for each question, so if you can't figure out an answer during the latter part of the section, just guess. Unlike other standardized tests such as the SAT, the GMAT will not penalize you for guessing.

OK, enough about time management. Now go ahead and start the final push for test day. Remember to time yourself and try to simulate the actual test environment when you take the full sets. If you notice anything bothering you during the test-taking session, write that down in your notebook and try to find a way to avoid the annoyance on test day. You have **75 minutes for the verbal part of the test and 75 minutes for the math part** of the test. On Review days, spend the full three to four hours reviewing the questions you highlighted before and the review techniques in your notebook and in the textbook. Participate in the online forums during the Review days if you feel that they are useful to you. You should also rest properly during this period, as taking these full sets can be stressful. And remember to keep your mind sharp and ready for the test that's coming up soon!

FINAL REVIEW: 3 DAYS BEFORE THE TEST

The final three days! Yay! We are almost there. There is only one thing that you should do in these final three days – review. You will easily forget any new information that you cram into your brain during these three days because you are too close to test day. Instead, focus on learning and relearning what you studied, and make sure that you understand all of the questions that you previously answered incorrectly. Go back to the techniques and quickly read through them to see if you've missed anything. Review your entire notebook and spend time on the most difficult subjects. Don't feel stressed about studying. Feel free to cut down on your study hours if you are comfortable with the topics. Use these three days to ready yourself mentally for the test and adjust your body to get ready for the test. And remember not to stay up late!

TEST DAY!

Finally, test day! Wake up early and have a good breakfast. Bring your notebook to the test center and quickly review it, but don't spend too much time trying to memorize everything. Take a deep breath before you start the test. Relax and enjoy the ride. Congratulations!

4

Section One: The Verbal Portion

For the rest of the book, we will look at the different sections to help you learn how to score high marks on the GMAT, and will try to understand how the test works and what you need to watch out for.

In this section, you will learn how to prepare for the verbal portion of the exam, what to look for, and how to ace this section.

If you think that you will find a guide that lists the answers to questions, or anything else that will make taking the test a piece of cake without having to study, then look elsewhere. This book is designed to help you in your study process. A lot of your success still comes down to you and your desire to take the exam, pass it with flying colors, get into a great business school, and start your long and successful career!

Taking the Verbal Portion

First things first. There are many ways that you can take the verbal test to make things easier on you as a whole. The following are just a few of the strategies that will help you stay relaxed and calm, which will help you properly answer the test questions. Remember:

STRESS IS THE ENEMY!

1. Organization is the key to passing the verbal portion of the GMAT. You are starting the test with the harder questions; this is where you need to shine, so work systematically to ensure that you put forth your best answers. Do not be afraid to scratch down thoughts to organize your thinking during the test. Look at the question with a rational mind and determine the answers that simply cannot fit. The first 15 questions on the GMAT verbal portion are the most important, as they will determine the overall flow and score of your test, so take your time with them. If you answer several of these questions in a row wrongly, you will start plummeting faster than a lead balloon. Stay calm and collected, work thoroughly on the questions in front of you, and do not panic.

2. Use the process of elimination when putting together the answers in your head. This is one of the most important techniques for taking the GMAT! By using this process, you will be surprised at how easy it is to eliminate the answer options that just don't belong. Instead of looking for the "right"

answer, "eliminate" the wrong answers from the choices and narrow down your options. Even if you can only eliminate one or two choices, your chance of guessing the right answer improves. So identify what's wrong with a choice, cross it off in your head or on a piece of paper, and do this for all of the answer choices to increase your chance of choosing the right answer.

3. Do not rush. Rushing is one of the worst things that you can do. If you are worried that you will fail or run out of time and, as a result, you race to finish the test, you will fail. Think about it this way. When you drive too fast down the road, is it easy to steer and navigate obstacles? No, it isn't. The same applies to the GMAT. If you race through the test, you will make mistakes, and those mistakes can cost you admission to an MBA program.

4. Some people find clocks distracting, especially during a test. The GMAT has a clock that you can turn off if you need to, so that you can focus on the test at hand.

5. There will be questions that you will have trouble answering, but that does not mean you should waste too much time on them. Answer them as best as you can. You have a 20% chance of answering them correctly, so why not try? Remember:

DON'T LEAVE A QUESTION UNANSWERED!

Also realize that some of the hard questions that you see on the tests are experimental and do not count towards your final scores.

6. Stay calm. This test is only a test and if you have studied hard, you will do fine. Do not get stressed out about it. Getting stressed, sweating, and panicking are the worst things that you can do. If you feel you are getting stressed out over the test, then just sit back, breathe, and take a moment—even a minute or two—to relax and refocus on the test.

5

Sentence Correction Questions

In most cases, sentence correction questions follow a standard format. A part of the question will be underlined, and you then use that to figure out what works best out of five different options. The first option will be the same as the original, while the other four will be different. Your task is to choose the option that best reflects the original question.

When you are trying to figure out the best option for your sentence, the following can help you decide on the correct answer.

- Go over the original question in your head. If you notice anything that doesn't sound right or natural, eliminate that answer, as the first answer choice is the same as the original question. You can also eliminate other answer choices that sound unnatural.

- Look for differences among the answers. Eliminate the answers with errors and settle on one, or at the very least, two options. It is very important that you don't second-guess yourself in this situation. Sometimes the same error will occur in multiple options. In this case, eliminate all of the options with the same error.

Understanding GMAT English

Thankfully, GMAT Sentence Corrections do not test everything regarding grammatical understanding, making things much easier on you. Here are the five rules that you need to understand when dealing with GMAT English.

1. If you took elementary English or even remember it, then you should know what a verb is. Essentially, a verb is related to a subject and describes the action related to the subject. For example:

   Layla ran home.

   In this situation, *Layla* is the subject and *ran* is the verb because it is an action that the subject is performing. Another example is this:

   Layla's house is burning.

   In this case, the subject is now *house*, while *burning* is the verb.

Attempt to understand how a verb agrees with its subject, either plural or singular. Remember that GMAT writers will catch many test takers on this rule, and the verb should agree with the subject. The test does this by separating the verb from the subject or by putting the verb before the subject.

For example:

a. *Each of the musicians (was, were) paid in advance*
b. *A series of Loch Ness Monster sightings (has, have) turned Scotland into a tourist destination.*
c. *There (is, are) a number of different ways to cook oysters.*

In the first example, since *Each* is singular because it refers to the individual musicians, *was* is the correct answer.

In the second example, *series* is always singular and is the subject, not *Loch Ness Monster sightings*. Therefore, *has* is the correct answer. Keep your eye out for tricks where subjects like *series, spate,* and *succession* are followed by prepositional phrases containing plurals. These subjects are still singular!

In the last example, *a number of different ways* is plural because it means *several*. Therefore, the correct answer is *are*.

2. The second grammatical rule that you need to follow on a GMAT is to make sure that pronouns refer to only one thing, and that the modifying phrase is as close as possible to what it is modifying. If a pronoun is underlined, find out what the pronoun is replacing, and is it singular used with singular, or

plural with plural? Also make sure that it is clear which noun the pronoun is replacing.

Before we get to the examples, let's quickly review pronouns. Essentially, a pronoun substitutes for a noun with or without a determiner (you, they, etc). Looking at the following sentence will make this much clearer:

Robert gave his steak to Mindy

In this case, all three nouns (*Robert, steak, Mindy*) can be replaced by pronouns; for example, *He gave it to her*. If Robert, the steak, and Mindy have all been mentioned before, then the reader can deduce what the pronouns *he*, *it*, and *her* refer to.

Other examples of sentences that use pronouns include:

- **Take it or leave it.**
- **I love you.**
- **She stared at them.**
- **That reminds me of him.**
- **Who says so?**

Let's look at two sample sentences to further understand this:

a. *The company promised to maintain operating factories inside the county, but (it, they) later reneged on the commitment.*
b. *If the couple cannot resolve their differences, the court will do (it, so).*

Company is a collective noun, as is *group*, *crowd*, etc., and requires a singular pronoun. Therefore, *it* is the correct answer.

In the second sentence, we do not know what *it* refers to. *It* could refer to custody of the children, the house, the car, and the terms—we simply do not know. Therefore, *so* is the correct answer.

Since we also mentioned modifiers in this rule, we will take a look at them in an example sentence. Modifiers are adjectives or adverbs with the ability to change the meaning of a noun, pronoun, or verb.

They laid his napkin (flat, flatly) on the table.

In the above example, the correct answer is *flat* because the modifier is referring to the *napkin* and not the verb *laid*.

3. The next rule is on parallel structure, and making sure that similar items in a list have a similar construction, and that only elements of the same sort are being compared.

No matter what nouns, verbs, or other elements are in a sentence, if they are of the same importance, they should be expressed the same way.

See the following samples to understand parallel structure.

The downward trend of the hockey team comes from mismanagement, poor performance, and (star players relocating, relocation of star players) to other teams.

The correct answer is *relocation of star players* because *mismanagement* and *performance* are nouns similar to *relocation.* If *mismanaging* and *performing* had been used in the sentence, then the correct answer would be *relocating.*

I remember my uncle making moonshine and (playing, that he would play) the banjo.

We are dealing with the word *making,* so the correct answer is *playing.*

To visualize excellence is not the same as (to achieve, achieving) it.

The correct answer is *to achieve* because *To visualize* is used instead of *visualizing.*

You can't compare apples to oranges, and you have to make sure that your comparisons are logically similar to each other. Remember that in parallel structures and comparisons, you can only compare similar words.

4. Using correct idioms can be difficult, and knowing the "right" way of saying something is not always easy. You might not be able to guess the meaning of an idiom as it is more along the lines of a figurative meaning and known only through common use. When you say, *He kicked the bucket,* people who speak the English language understand that he did not literally kick the bucket, but that he died.

Let's look at a few examples:

a. *Wayne Gretzky is regarded (as, to be) one of the greatest*

NHL hockey players.

b. *Pollution from greenhouse gases is generally (considered, considered as, considered to be) a major threat to the environment.*

c. *It took me twice as long to build the shed collaboratively (as, than) it would have taken by myself.*

Idioms can also be used in comparison and, as a result, must be followed by parallel constructions.

d. *Neil Young is not just a great singer, (and also, but also, but is also) a legendary musical icon.*

Looking at the first example, the correct answer is *as.*

The correct answer for the second example is *considered*. Although *considered to be* is also grammatically correct, it will not be considered correct on the GMAT.

As is correct in the third example, because *as long* was used earlier in the sentence. You use *than* when it is preceded by an -er word, while you use *as* when it is preceded by *as.*

The last statement uses *but also* because the format for a parallel construction is *not only ... but also ....*

5. Do not use unnecessary words and avoid redundancy. Also, do not use passive verbs if you can avoid doing so.

Many errors come from using an ineffective expression and problems with style. The most common of these on the GMAT is the use of far too many verbs to get the point across. The common problems are: too many words meaning the same thing, redundancy, or using a passive voice when the sentence needs an active verb.

Let's look at these sentences and see how they could be rewritten.

a. *There are many children who believe in the Easter Bunny, but there are few adults who do.*
b. *The largest pyramid is at least 4,000 years old or older.*
c. *The Lord of the Rings has been bought and read by millions of readers since it was first published in 1951.*

The first sentence could read as *Many children believe in the Easter Bunny, but few adults do.* Repeating *there is/are* makes sentences too wordy.

In the second sentence, saying *at least* and *or older* is redundant. *At least* implies that the minimum age is 4,000, so it may be much older. The sentence should read as *The largest pyramid is at least 4,000 years old.*

The third sentence should read *Millions of readers have enjoyed The Lord of the Rings since it was first published in 1951.* In the sentence, *has been* is in a passive voice and should be avoided.

Things to Remember...

Always start by examining the question carefully. Try your best to find errors and problems with the original sentence before looking at the answer choices. If you find an error in the original sentence, go to the answer choices and eliminate all of the choices that contain the same error. If you don't see an error in the original sentence, proceed to the choices and decide whether the original sentence is the best choice. Don't try to fix the original sentence if it's not broken!

Always put your final choice into the question sentence and double-check whether there are any errors that you hadn't noticed before.

As mentioned above, when you find an error in a sentence, eliminate all choices that contain that same error either in the original question or in any of the choices. Use the process of elimination to save you time and avoid confusion.

The three basic elements of any sentence are subject, verb, and object. Always know where these three elements are so that you have a good understanding of the structure of a sentence. First check for consistency among these three elements and make sure that they all agree with each other. Subject, verb, and object are often separated by phrases so pay attention to them throughout the entire sentence.

Understand that idioms don't follow any rules. The best way to deal with idioms is to simply memorize them. Throughout your practice sessions, make a list of the idioms that you are not familiar with and review the list frequently.

When you see a sentence with parallel components, which are usually created by the use of "and," "or," "but," "similar to," "in contrast to," "as well as," "like," "unlike," and others, make sure that the parallel components are consistent in grammatical structure.

A pronoun is a word that replaces a noun. Words such as *he*, *she*, *it*, *who*, are pronouns. When a pronoun is unclear, meaning that you cannot be sure of the noun to which it refers, or if the pronoun could refer to multiple nouns, then an error exists.

Avoid the passive voice if possible. The passive voice is usually not as clear as the active voice, which is generally more effective. That said, using the passive voice does not create a grammatical error, and if no grammatically correct alternative exists, then consider the passive voice. The passive voice can also be used when it is impossible or inappropriate to state the subject of the action.

If omitting words/phrases makes the sentence unclear, the words/phrases should not have been omitted and should be put back in. On the other hand, the phrase *to be* is often unnecessary, so when you see it in a sentence, check the sentence for other unnecessary words.

Understand the difference between *greater* and *more*, and between *fewer* and *less*. *Greater* is used when describing numbers while *more* is used when describing a number of things. For example, the number of people in the classroom is *greater* than 20; there are *more* than 20 people in the classroom. For *fewer* and *less*, use *fewer* if you can count the objects, and use *less* if the objects are not countable. For example, *fewer* apples and *less* air. The same rule applies to *number* and *amount*, where *number* is used for countable objects and *amount* is used for uncountable objects. For example, the *number* of participants and the *amount* of effort. One quick note: *numbers* can be counted but *percentages* cannot. For example, *fewer than 30* people showed up; *less than 30 percent of the people showed up.*

Eliminate an answer choice immediately if you find a grammatical error. Although this section asks you to consider the effectiveness of the choices, the correct choice will never contain a grammatical error. On the other hand, don't expect to always find the perfect answer, as the point is to pick the best choice among the answer choices provided, and not the perfect one.

6

Reading Comprehension

Reading for the GMAT is easy once you understand how passages are constructed. This part of the GMAT primarily tests your ability to understand main ideas in a short article. The passages are all of the same style, and you'll be very familiar with that style after you've answered the questions a couple of times. Don't try to understand every little detail in the passages and remember that the goal is not to understand everything stated but to find the right answer choice!

The Scope of the Text

There is a common saying: *Can't see the forest for the trees.* This applies to evaluating the text in the Reading Comprehension part of the GMAT. When you first read the passage, you need to look at it from afar before analyzing its details. Pay attention to the scope of the passage and try to understand its overall intent. After you have a good idea of its scope, you can start analyzing it deeper.

Break it Down

Now that you have looked at the entire concept of the passage as a whole, begin to break everything down into smaller parts.

When you begin to break it down, it is very important that you do not break down every single piece of the passage simply because you are worried about missing something.

Critical reading is not about analyzing everything. Remember, writers do not put meaning into everything they write, but only into a few pieces of text that need to be noticed. You should look for important sentences, and you will find other sentences that are secondary but help you understand the concept of the passage.

Sadly, you don't have a lot of time to go over the passages, analyze them, pick out the good points and the bad points, and understand the concepts. After all, the test is timed, so you have to work quickly and efficiently.

Here are a few tips that should help you.

- Not all sentences are equal. Some are important, while others are not. Identifying which is which will help you a lot.

- Only glance over the secondary and pointless details of a passage.
- Focus on the topic sentence in each paragraph.
- Read the important stuff very carefully to fully understand it.

Things to Remember...

To quickly answer most of the questions, make sure that you understand the key points of the article and the reason why the article was written. Keep these in mind when you read the passage. Do not get sucked into trying to figure out the details. Grasp the main ideas first. And read the entire passage, as the main idea and key points may not be obvious unless you do so.

Always quickly scan the entire passage to get a rough idea of what it is about. Then create a mental image of how the passage is structured and the key points in each paragraph. Do not try to memorize details but try to summarize the key points of each paragraph into one or two sentences. As long as you understand the structure of the passage and know that you can find information, you can always go back to sift through the details if necessary. Again:

1. Scan the passage;
2. Grasp the main ideas and key points;
3. Understand the paragraph structure;

4. Go back to find details only when a question requires details.

Spend no more than five minutes reading the passage and roughly one minute per question. Since some passages are long, be sure that you are comfortable with the speed at which you read them.

Read the questions carefully and don't be confused by answer choices that contain the same words or phrases as those in the passage. This is a common trap used in Reading Comprehension questions to trick you into selecting the wrong answer. Pay attention to the meaning of the answer choices and not how the sentence is constructed.

If the passage contains a lot of technical terms (for example, scientific language), do not panic! The GMAT does not require you to have any knowledge in specific fields. All of the information you need is in the question. There is no need to panic. Attack these passages with the same tactics as you use for other passages and get a firm understanding of the key points and the structure of the paragraphs.

Understand that the information needed to answer questions containing references to a line are not far from that particular line in the passage. This is also why you don't have to memorize details but can instead refer to the passage to find the information you need.

Pay extra attention if you see a question or answer choice that uses information from different parts of the passage, as this is a common trap. Most of the time, the information needed to answer the question will be near that part of the passage. So, answer choices using information from different parts of the passage are likely not the correct answer.

7

Critical Reasoning on the GMAT

Critical Reasoning is a favorite of people who love to argue. Here, your talents at arguing, breaking apart reasoning, and finding weak points to attack or defend will shine.

This section is one of the most important on the GMAT. Anyone who can argue persuasively by logically evaluating an issue on its merits and responding to its strength and weaknesses has the critical thinking needed to be a good business manager.

Business managers must evaluate arguments and proposals with a critical eye because not all business deals recognize their parties equally. Sometimes you have to argue your point to be heard.

This section accounts for a full 30% of your verbal section score, and contains about 12 to 13 questions.

Understanding Critical Reasoning Questions

To answer questions correctly in this section, it is very important to identify the various parts of critical reasoning questions.

The Question

Critical reasoning questions are easy to understand as they are very short and usually come in the form of: *For each question, select the best of the answer choices given.* A critical aspect to answering the questions lies in the instruction itself. Note that you are not told to select the *perfect* answer, but to select the *best* answer available from the choices given.

The Short Passage

The next part of the question is the short passage. The passage is drawn from a variety of areas, including casual conversation, natural sciences, and more. You may have no experience with the topic, but that is okay, as you do not need outside knowledge to understand the question. Just understand the question based on the information provided. The question may ask you what will strengthen or weaken the argument, or to make a deduction from the passage.

Choosing the right answer can be difficult, especially when some questions have two or more correct answers. Here are a few steps that can help.

1. Before you read the short passage, read and understand the question as thoroughly as possible because your understanding of the short passage will depend on the question. If you know what you are supposed to look for before reading the short passage, you will be able to take a more logical approach while reading.

2. Once you understand the question, read the short passage. Most critical reasoning questions require you to identify parts of the argument, so read the passage actively and critically. Understanding the strength or weakness of the argument will help you answer the question.

3. Since you know the question and have read the passage, do yourself a lot of good by first answering the question without looking at the answers provided. For example, if the question wants you to find a statement to weaken the argument, review the passage and determine what could weaken it.

4. If you determined an answer, then look at the answers provided for a match. If you couldn't come up with an answer, skim through each answer provided, keeping the passage in mind. Quickly eliminate the answers that do not apply. Once you select an answer, reread the question and the passage to be certain about your answer.

Splitting Up the Argument

Of course, reading a passage and drawing your own conclusions is one thing. Reading the answers and figuring out the best one for question in relation to the passage is another thing altogether.

For Critical Reasoning, understanding the argument is most important for answering the questions. Doing this involves identifying the different components of the passage. On the GMAT, the argument is a claim supported by reasoning.

The Earth is flat because it looks flat.

This was a common argument centuries ago, and it carries the same components that an author uses when pushing across his or her argument. What are these components?

1. The conclusion: This is the author's claim or the point that he or she is trying to make. In this example, *The Earth is flat* is the conclusion.

2. The evidence: This is what the author uses to back up his or her claim. Here, *It looks flat* is the evidence.

While reading these questions, it is important that you identify the conclusion from the evidence provided. First, despite its name, the conclusion by no means comes at the end of a passage. It may come at the beginning, it may follow the evidence, or it may in fact be at the end.

As a result, finding the conclusion in a long passage can be difficult. Thankfully, a few keywords can ease the process. *Therefore, Thus, As a result, Hence, Clearly, So,* and *Consequently* are examples of conclusion keywords. We know this because their meaning essentially signals the beginning of a conclusion.

> *When I look around I see flatness, (Therefore, Thus, As a Result, Hence, So, Consequently) the Earth is flat.*
>
> *Clearly the Earth is flat because all I see around me is flat ground.*

These two sentences show how conclusion keywords signal the conclusion.

Evidence keywords help you identify the evidence. *Because, Since,* and *For* are examples of evidence keywords.

> *The world is flat because all I see is flat ground around me.*
>
> *Since all I see around me is flat ground, the Earth is therefore flat.*
>
> *The Earth is flat for all I see around me is flat ground.*

Obviously, this is a very easy question to answer correctly because it contains just one line, one quick piece of evidence, and one quick conclusion. However, searching for evidence keywords can be effective for longer passages. The following sample passage helps us understand how.

> *Global warming is a serious problem for our planet. All around us, the Earth is heating up to record temperatures, which can seriously affect our way of life. Since global warming became a problem after the advent of the automobile, it can clearly be ascertained that the invention of the automobile has caused global warming. Only the elimination of the automobile will then fix the problem of global warming.*

This relatively long passage includes some fluff and secondary points. Where is the evidence and conclusion? Let's look again, with the keywords underlined.

> *Global warming is a serious problem for our planet. All around us, the Earth is heating up to record temperatures, which can seriously affect our way of life. Since global warming became a problem after the advent of the automobile, it can clearly be ascertained that the invention of the automobile has caused global warming. Only the elimination of the automobile will then fix the problem of global warming.*

Now we see why identifying an easy passage like *The earth is flat because all I see is flat ground* is such an effective tool to use to figure out a passage. While reading the above passage, take out everything that is not needed and condense it into a short sentence that includes the evidence and the conclusion.

If done properly, your short sentence should read something like this.

> *Since global warming became a problem after the automobile was invented, it is clear that is the cause of global warming.*

We have taken a complicated passage and condensed it into a short sentence, eliminating the useless information. Doing this leads you to see the conclusion and evidence quickly and easily.

Now that we have covered the scope of the questions and how they can be broken up into smaller bits to help you to make an informed decision, we will move on to the types of questions that you will be asked on the GMAT.

Assumption Questions

The first type of question is the assumption question. In this question, the author makes an assumption about something, and it is up to you to select the best of the answers provided based on that assumption.

First, find anything that goes beyond the scope of the argument. Often, each argument is written within a narrow set of parameters. The wrong answers go beyond these simple parameters.

Second, wrong answers to assumption questions often use extreme language that goes beyond the claim of the author.

Lastly, wrong answers do not support the argument. Remember, an assumption must support the argument, and an assumption must be true for the argument to be valid.

To determine where the author is going with the assumption, ask yourself the following questions.

- Which of the following, if added to the passage, makes the conclusion more valid?
- Which of the following does the author assume?
- The validity of the argument depends on which of the following?

Strengthening and Weakening Questions

This is the most common type of critical thinking question that you will face on the GMAT. Obviously, these questions are pretty easy to understand. You need to analyze what may strengthen or weaken the argument made by the author.

As with the previous type of question, and any other critical thinking question on the GMAT, break the passage apart to determine what will strengthen or weaken the argument.

When trying to strengthen the argument, pick out the choice that will best fill in the key assumption and give it more merit. When you want to weaken an argument, pick the choice that will undercut the key assumption.

Flaw Questions

These questions are far less common than strengthening and weakening questions, and assumption questions, but there is a chance that you will see at least one on the GMAT.

Flaw questions are often presented in one of the following ways:

- The argument is flawed in that it ignores the possibility of...
- Which of the following points is the most serious logical flaw in the argument?
- Which of the following would reveal most of the absurdity of the conclusion?

Do not confuse flaw questions with weakens questions. Although they may seem similar, in weakens questions you are supposed to find additional information to weaken the argument if it is true. In a flaw question, the evidence is not very supportive of the conclusion, and you as the test taker must explain why.

As usual, break up the argument to find out how best to determine why it is flawed.

Inference Questions

There will be a few inference questions on the test. These questions do not make it necessary for you to distinguish the evidence from the conclusion when you read the passage. In fact, you can treat the entire passage as evidence and draw your own conclusion.

The inference question may be worded in many different ways, including:

- The facts above best support which conclusion?
- Which of the following conclusions can be properly drawn from the information above?
- If the statements above are true, what conclusion can be based on them?
- If the statements above are true, which of the following below are true as well?

Explanation Questions

The last form of question that you will find on the GMAT is an explain question. These questions are completely different from the other types of questions for the very reason that they present no argument. Instead, the passage, which usually contains the argument, will describe a situation with two or more contradictory facts. Answering the question means explaining how the two contradictory facts can actually be true. You will find that incorrect answer choices:

- Touch upon only one fact;
- Make the decision even more ambiguous;
- Make a pointless comparison;
- Fail to address the scope.

Things to Remember...

Pay attention to the assumptions, evidence, and conclusion for each question. The questions are likely to be long and relate to complicated sentence structures. Don't let that distract you from understanding the argument presented by the question. The conclusion should be supported by factual evidence, while the assumptions need to be true if the conclusion and the entire argument are to be solid.

All facts not stated in the question should be treated as assumptions. Remember that the GMAT does not require you to have knowledge in any specific field, and you shouldn't have to use any knowledge/facts related to specific fields when answering any questions. Therefore, treat any knowledge that you obtained outside of the test as assumptions that need to be qualified before you can use them as facts when answering questions.

How do you know if an assumption is necessary? One quick way to find out is by denying the assumption and determining whether the argument still holds. If the argument falls apart, the assumption is necessary and cannot be omitted or changed.

On questions regarding percentages and ratios, be careful not to confuse ratios with numbers and quantities. If ratios confuse you, assigning actual numbers to the ratios may help. For example, if the question says "56% of American people," first assume that the entire population consists of 100 million people and then convert "56% of American people" into "56 million American people." Be careful of the new assumption that you made, and make sure that it does not conflict with the statements in the question.

Pay extra attention when presented with a survey or with research, as these often test you on how to draw the correct conclusion from them. Examine all assumptions carefully and make sure that the groups represented in the results are the same, or are at least similar to some extent.

Watch for a question that changes the scope of an argument. The question may draw general conclusions about an entire group from a specific smaller group. Be careful about generalization.

Make sure that you understand the difference between causation and correlation. Correlation indicates that a relationship exists between two things but it does not specify cause and effect. Just because something happens before another does not automatically make it the cause. Also keep in mind that sometimes one piece of evidence can be the cause for multiple possible outcomes, and one particular outcome can have more than one cause.

8

GMAT Math

If you are planning on attending business school, then you are most likely very familiar with the math that you will see on the GMAT. In fact, if you went to junior high school, then you have studied this kind of math. The GMAT mainly tests your knowledge of arithmetic, algebra, and geometry, and no other complicated math concepts. You may breathe a sigh of relief now.

The math portion of the GMAT is not as difficult as you may think. Certain types of questions come up on every test, and they are expressed the same way each time. You could say that some of the words and phrasing are predictable.

Here is what you can expect as question topics from the GMAT math portion:

- Adding, subtracting, multiplying, and dividing fractions;
- Converting fractions to decimals;
- Adding, subtracting, multiplying, and dividing signed numbers;
- Putting numbers into algebraic expressions;
- Finding a percent using the percentage formula;
- Finding an average;

- Finding the areas of rectangles, triangles, and circles.

Without further hesitation, let's move on to the math portion of the GMAT.

Things to Remember...

The following are three very important tools for solving GMAT math questions:

1. Backsolving;
2. Assigning values;
3. "Drawing" the questions (for word problems).

Backsolving is a method for testing the answer choices given to you for a question. Basically, select one of the five choices, and then put the choice into the question to see if it is correct. If it is not correct, eliminate the choice and pick another one. You've found the correct answer if the choice correctly solves the math problem! This is a simple and effective way to solve math questions, especially when you don't know how to solve the question directly. An additional trick: if the answer choices are concrete values, try the middle value first. Depending on the question, you may be able to determine whether you should next try values larger or smaller than the middle value.

Assigning values is similar to backsolving in that you are trying to find the answer without directly solving the question. Basically, assign specific values to undefined values in the questions, and then look at the answer choices to see which one makes sense. For example, if the question asks about integers, pick a few integers and plug them into the question. This makes working with variables and unknowns much easier. The values you assign should be easy to work with. With practice, you'll know what values to use for different questions. Assigning values will not directly give you an answer but will help you understand the question better and make choosing an answer easier.

The math required to answer word problems is usually easier than that needed for straight math problems, but the added language means that you need a clear understanding of the questions. Understanding the questions is one of the most important keys to correctly answering these word problems. I found it useful to draw these word problems out on a piece of paper, as this helps me think clearly without getting tangled up in the words and sentences, and complicated word problems can be converted into simple math problems by doing this. To do this, carefully read the entire question and identify the variables. Then draw the situation on paper to put a clear context to it and to conceptualize the question. Finally, translate the question into a math problem by turning sentences into equations. This is especially useful for questions related to geometry, ratio, speed, rate, distance, and volume.

Arithmetic

Expect to deal with arithmetic in some form or another during the math portion of the GMAT. As a result, you will need to understand basic arithmetic definitions.

Numbers

The following are the different kinds of numbers that appear on the GMAT.

- Real numbers are numbers on the number line. All of the numbers used on the GMAT are real numbers.
- Rational numbers are numbers expressed as the ratio of two integers, and include all integers and fractions.
- Irrational numbers are real numbers that are not rational, meaning that they can be either positive or negative.
- Integers are numbers with no fractional or decimal areas. They are all multiples of one.

Operations

Operations essentially dictate how the entire mathematical sequence reads on paper. Operations include everything from parenthesis and exponents to simple arithmetic expressions.

The order for operations is as follows:

- Parentheses;
- Exponents;

- Multiplication / Division (from left to right);
- Addition / Subtraction (from left to right).

Let's look at a sample equation that requires you to follow the above order:

$$27 + 5 \times 4 + (100 / 5) - 19 = ?$$

If we don't follow the order, and just work from left to right, the answer is 26.6.

However, doing it in correct operation order yields the following:

1. Solve the numbers in the parenthesis first: 100 / 5 = 20
2. Do the multiplication and division from left to right: 5 x 4 = 20
3. Now the formula is as follows: 27 + 20 + 20 – 19
4. Now do the addition and subtraction from left to right
5. This yields the result of 48.

This answer is a bit different from the answer we got by not following the order of the operations.

Law of Operations

You should remember the following mathematics laws and their operations so that you can correctly do the calculations.

Commutative Law

Addition and multiplication are commutative. This means that no matter what order they are done in, the result is the same.

$$10 + 15 = 25$$

$$15 + 10 = 25$$

$$9 \times 2 = 18$$

$$2 \times 9 = 18$$

Division and subtraction, however, are not commutative.

$$9 - 2 = 7$$

$$2 - 9 = -7$$

$$10 / 2 = 5$$

$$2 / 10 = .2$$

Associative Law

Addition and multiplication, as above, are also associative. This means that these operations can be regrouped in any way without changing the end result. Division and subtraction, on the other hand, are not associative.

$(10 + 10) + 9 = 10 + (10 + 9)$

$20 + 9 = 10 + 19$

$29 = 29$

$(5 \times 5) \times 2 = 5 \times (2 \times 5)$

$25 \times 2 = 5 \times 10$

$50 = 50$

Distributive Law

Distributive law allows you to distribute a factor among the terms that are added or subtracted, often seen as a(b+c) = ab + ac.

$$4(10 + 2) = 4 \times 10 + 4 \times 2$$

$$4 \times 12 = 40 + 8$$

$$48 = 48$$

Division can be done in a similar format.

$$(3 + 5) / 2 = 3 / 2 + 5 /2$$

$$8 / 2 = 3 /2 + 5 /2$$

$$4 = 1.5 + 2. 5$$

$$4 = 4$$

Fractions

Fractions form a significant portion of the math portion of the GMAT. Let's review the basics of fractions, such as:

$$\frac{3}{5}$$

3 is the numerator, with the fraction bar below, meaning divided by, and

5 is the denominator.

Of course, there is more to remember than simply numerator and denominator. So let's get into the different types of fractions.

Equivalent Fractions

In this type of fraction, its fractional value remains unchanged when you multiply it by one. When dealing with fractions, multiplying the numerator and denominator by the same non-zero number is equivalent to multiplying them by one; the fractional value remains unchanged. You also get the same result when dividing by the same non-zero number.

$$\frac{1}{2}=\frac{1\times3}{2\times3}=\frac{3}{6}$$

$$\frac{6}{9}=\frac{6\div3}{9\div3}=\frac{2}{3}$$

Canceling and Reducing

When dealing with fractions, especially on the GMAT, you have to work to put fractions in the lowest terms. This means that the numerator and denominator cannot be divisible by any other common integer except for one.

The best way to think about this is to look at 6/24. This fraction can be reduced by dividing both the numerator and the denominator by 3, to get 2/8. We can divide the numerator and denominator once more by 2, and get ¼.

An example of a question that you will face on the GMAT concerning this is this as follows:

Reduce $\frac{50}{110}$ to its lowest terms.

To do this, divide by 5 to get $\frac{10}{22}$.

At this point, divide by 2 to get $\frac{5}{11}$.

Addition and Subtraction

You can add or subtract two fractions only if they have the same denominator. We first need to find the common denominator, which is often called the lowest common denominator. It is a significant concept to understanding with respect to fractions.

$$\frac{4}{5}+\frac{1}{3}-\frac{3}{4}$$

Here, the denominators are 5, 3, and 4. To find the lowest common denominator, multiply the denominators and numerators of each fraction by the values that give the common denominator.

lowest common denominator = 5 x 3 x 4 = 60

Therefore, we now do this operation to turn everything into the required common denominator:

$$\left(\frac{4}{5}\times\frac{12}{12}\right)+\left(\frac{1}{3}\times\frac{20}{20}\right)+\left(\frac{3}{4}\times\frac{15}{15}\right)$$

This then gives us:

$$\frac{48}{60}+\frac{20}{60}-\frac{45}{60}$$

Now, all we have to do is add the numerators together over the common denominator.

$$\frac{48+20-45}{60}=\frac{23}{60}$$

Multiplication

With fractions, multiplication is different from addition and subtraction. First, no common denominator needs to be in place for multiplication to work. For multiplication, you simply need to reduce both diagonally and vertically, and then multiply numerators together and denominators together.

$$\frac{5}{9}\times\frac{3}{4}\times\frac{8}{15}$$

This is reduced to:

$$\frac{1}{3}\times\frac{1}{1}\times\frac{2}{3}$$

Then, multiply it all together:

$$\frac{1\times1\times2}{3\times1\times3}$$

which then equals $\frac{2}{9}$.

Division

Division works just like multiplication and, in fact, all you do is multiply the reciprocal of the divisor. To get this, invert the fraction by changing the position of the numerator and denominator. Let's look at an example:

$$\frac{4}{3}\div\frac{4}{9}$$

We first have to invert the reciprocal to $\frac{4}{9}$, which then turns the equation into:

$$\frac{4}{3}\div\frac{9}{4}$$

But since we are not dividing but multiplying, the equation now looks like this:

$$\frac{4}{3} \times \frac{9}{4}$$

We then reduce this to:

$$\frac{1}{1} \times \frac{3}{1}$$

which turns into:

$$\frac{1 \times 3}{1 \times 1}$$

which equals 3.

Decimal Fractions

Decimal fractions are simply fractions in decimal form. To find the decimal form of a fraction, multiply to the power of ten in the denominator.

In addition, each digit in the decimal has a name. The GMAT will sometimes test you on this, so here is a quick guide. For example,

527.236

5 = the hundreds digit

2 = the tens digit

7 = the units digit

.

2 = the tenths digit

3 = the hundredths digit

6 = the thousandths digit

Now, let's look at examples of how to change decimal fractions into actual fractions using an example question from the GMAT.

Arrange in order from smallest to largest: 0.5, 0.55, 0.05, 0.505 and 0.055

$$.5 = .500 = \frac{500}{1000}$$

$$.55 = .550 = \frac{550}{1000}$$

$$.05 = .050 = \frac{50}{1000}$$

$$.505 = .505 = \frac{505}{1000}$$

$$.055 = .055 = \frac{55}{1000}$$

Therefore, the order should be: .05 < .055 < .5 < .505 < .55.

When adding or subtracting these, make sure that all of the decimal points line up properly, one on top of the other. This will ensure that the tenths add with the tenths, the hundredths add with the hundredths, and so on.

Let's look at this example:

$$.9 + .09 + .009$$

In this case, we will convert it into vertical form:

$$\begin{array}{r} 0.9 \\ +\ 0.09 \\ +\ \underline{0.009} \\ 0.999 \end{array}$$

The same holds true when subtracting, so whenever using addition or subtraction, always remember to line up the decimal points to ensure that you get the proper answers.

In terms of multiplication, multiply as you would with any other integer. Then decide where the decimal point should be. The number of decimal places for the answer equals the sum of the number of decimal places from each of the two decimals you are multiplying together.

For example:

$$0.5 \times 0.3 = 0.15$$

$$1.2 \times 1.7 = 2.04$$

When dividing a decimal with another decimal, multiply each by the power of 10 so that the divisor becomes an integer. Then, simply carry out the division as you would with integers, placing the decimal point in the quotient directly above the decimal point in the dividend.

For example:

$$8 \div 0.4 =$$

$$(8 \times 10) \div (0.4 \times 10) =$$

$$80 \div 4 = 20$$

9

NUMBER PROPERTIES

For the GMAT, you need to learn many different concepts related to numbers . Some are easy and others are hard. Regardless of whether easy or difficult, we will cover them here for you in an effort to provide explanations and to help you pass the math questions on the test.

Number Line and Absolute Value

What is a number line? Plainly put, it is a line of numbers. That may seem obvious, but sometimes needs explanation.

A number line will extend infinitely in two directions, one continuously toward infinity and the other continuously toward negative infinity. In other words, as you move to the right on the number line, values become larger. The farther you move to the left on the number line, the smaller the numbers become.

Zero separates the positive numbers from the negative numbers. For example, there is 3 and there is –3, there is 12 and there is –12, there is 1,385,388,905 and there is –1,385,388,905.

What is an absolute value?

The absolute value of any number is the number without its negative sign. It is written simply as two vertical lines. The absolute value of a number can be thought of as the distance from zero on the number line.

An example of this is $|-5| = |+5| = 5$

Look at it this way: –5 is 5 units from zero, so its absolute value is 5.

Properties of -1, 0, 1 and Other Numbers

What are the properties of zero? Can zero have properties or is it simply the lack of everything, a void, and therefore without properties. Well, the good news is that it can have properties and we will cover them here, along with the properties of some other numbers.

It is common knowledge that adding or subtracting zero from any number does not change the value of the number. This is simple basic math:

$$0 + 7 = 7$$

$$9 + 0 = 9$$

$$8 - 0 = 0$$

Now, the rules change when you multiply by zero. In this case, the result of any number multiplied by zero is zero. See the following examples:

$$25 \times 0 = 0$$

$$198 \times 0 = 0$$

Dividing by zero cannot be done. If you put that sort of equation into your calculator, you will get an error.

Now that we have looked into the properties of 0, what about 1 and –1?

Well, multiplying or dividing any number by 1 does not change that number. Again, this is basic elementary school math.

$$7 \div 1 = 7$$

$$9 \times 1 = 9$$

$$-17 \times 1 = -17$$

Things change slightly when we begin to multiply by –1. In this case, doing so changes the sign of the number we are multiplying. Let's look at some examples.

$$Z \times (-1) = -Z$$

$$9 \times (-1) = -9$$

$$-6 \div (-1) = 6$$

When we look at the reciprocal of a number, we simply look at it as 1 divided by that number. With fractions, the reciprocal is found by interchanging the denominator and the numerator, and cover the values between –1 and 1. Moreover, the reciprocal of a number between 0 and 1 is greater than the number. Here are some examples:

The reciprocal of $\frac{3}{4}$ is: $1 / (\frac{3}{4}) = \frac{4}{3} = 1\frac{1}{3}$. As we can see, this figure is larger than the original number.

Conversely, the reciprocal of a number between 0 and 1 is less than the number:

$$-(\frac{2}{3}) : 1 / -(\frac{2}{3}) = -(\frac{3}{2}) = -1\frac{1}{2}$$

For the square of a number, when it is a square of a number between 0 and 1, it is less than that number.

$$(\frac{1}{3})^2 = \frac{1}{3} \times \frac{1}{3} = \frac{1}{9}$$

Multiplying any negative number by a fraction between 0 and 1 will result in a number greater than the original number.

$$-7 \times \frac{1}{5} = -\frac{7}{5}$$

Operations and Signed Numbers

We looked at operations in a previous part of the book, and now it is time to review them again. This time, we are looking at signed numbers and how a different form of operations is used on them.

For addition of numbers of similar signs, we simply add them and keep the sign:

$$-9 + -2 = -11$$

However, if we are dealing with numbers of different signs, then we take the difference of the absolute values and keep the sign of the larger absolute value.

$$(-9) + (+3) = -6$$

Subtraction is the opposite of addition. Subtracting a number is the same as adding its inverse to it. Many people find subtraction easier than addition.

$$(-4) - (-8) = (-4) + (+8) = +4$$

In multiplication and division, the product or the quotient of the two numbers with the same sign is positive. Here is an example:

$$(-3) \times (-4) = +12$$

$$-100 / -50 = +2$$

The product or the quotient of two numbers with opposite signs is negative:

$$(-4) \times (+3) = -12$$

$$-100 / 50 = -2$$

Odd and Even Numbers

Odd and even numbers only apply to integers. The best way to remember odd and even numbers is that even numbers are integers divisible by 2, while odd numbers are not divisible by 2.

Any number that ends in 0, 2, 4, 6, or 8 are even, while integers ending in 1, 3, 5, 7, or 9 are odd. Negative numbers can also be odd or even. Zero is considered an even number.

When dealing with operations for odd and even numbers, there are some simple rules to follow:

Odd + Odd = Even

Even + Even = Even

Odd + Even = Odd

Odd x Odd = Odd

Even x Even = Even

Odd x Even = Even

Factors and Divisibility of Primes

Any integer divisible by another integer is effectively a multiple of that integer:

16 is a multiple of 4 because 16 / 4 = 4; 4 x 4 = 16

In division, when you are dealing with a remainder, the remainder is always smaller than the number we are dividing by.

17 divided by 3 is 5, and the remainder is 2

A factor is a divisor of a number that can evenly divide into that integer.

9 has 3 factors: 1, 3, 9

1 x 9 = 9; 3 x 3 = 9

When talking about the greatest common factor, mathematics is talking about the largest factor that can be shared by two numbers.

One great thing about factors is that you can do divisibility tests to see if the number is divisible by 2, 3, 4, 5, 6, and 9. Here are the rules:

Any number can be divided by 2 if the last digit is divisible by 2.

224 is divisible by 2 because 4 is divisible by 2.

If the sum of all of the digits of a number is divisible by 3, then the entire number is divisible by 3.

135 is divisible by 3 because 1 + 3 + 5 = 9.

A number is divisible by four if its last two digits are divisible by 4.

1,240 is divisible by 4 because 40 is divisible by 4.

A number is divisible by 5 if its last digit is a 0 or a 5.

2,517,545 is divisible by 5.

A number is divisible by 6 if it is divisible by BOTH 2 and 3.

4,422 is divisible by 6 because the last digit is divisible by 2, and the sum of all of its digits is 12, which is divisible by 3.

A number is divisible by 9 if the sum of the digits is divisible by 9, much like how the division rule for 3 works.

14,832 is divisible by 9 because 1 + 4 + 8 + 3 + 2 = 18, which is divisible by 9.

Now that we are past that, let's move on to prime numbers. A prime number is any integer greater than 1 that can only be divided by 1 and itself. The first prime number is 2, and is the only even prime number. Here is a quick list of the first ten prime numbers: 2, 3, 5, 7, 11, 13, 17, 19, 23, and 29.

Prime factorization of a number is the expression of the number as a product of prime factors. A related rule that never changes is that no matter how you factor a number, its prime factors will always be the same.

$$92 = 2 \times 2 \times 23$$

$$923112 = 2 \times 2 \times 2 \times 3 \times 3 \times 12821$$

$$224 = 2 \times 2 \times 2 \times 2 \times 2 \times 7$$

Determining the prime factorization for a number is difficult, but there is an easy way to determine it. Let's look at this example:

$$150 = 10 \times 15 = 2 \times 5 \text{ and } 5 \times 3 = 2 \times 5 \times 5 \times 3$$

Consecutive Numbers

If the numbers in a list are at a fixed interval, then they are consecutive numbers. They need to have a pattern to be considered consecutive numbers. Also, all consecutive numbers that you encounter on the exam will be integers.

1, 2, 3, 4, 5… is consecutive in intervals of +1, adding up

2, 0, –2, –4, –6… is consecutive in intervals of –2, subtracting down

2, 4, 8, 16, 32… is a consecutive in intervals of squaring

10

AVERAGES

If you love sports and watch them on a regular basis, then you know all about averages. A frequently used average is a pitcher's earned run average (E.R.A.), which is calculated by adding up all of the runs that a pitcher had in the innings he pitched, and then dividing that by the number of innings. For example, if a pitcher had 47 runs in 19 innings pitched, then his E.R.A is 2.47 (47 / 19 = 2.47).

Averages are easy to calculate, as they are simply the sum of values divided by the number of values used.

Here is an example:

Craig is 180 pounds, Jim is 201 pounds, and Francis is 257 pounds. What is the average weight of the three men?

$$180 + 201 + 257 = 638$$

$$638 / 3 = 212.67$$

The average weight is 212.67 pounds.

Finding the average is easy, but can you find the sum of the values with nothing but the average and the number of values? Well, this is also easy, since we have two of the variables we need to find the solution.

$$\text{Sum of Values} = \text{Average Value} \times \text{Number of Values}$$

$$212.67 \times 3 = 638$$

It is that easy to figure that out, as long as you have the two variables – average value and number of values – to complete the equation.

When looking at a series of numbers, with only the average known, how do we solve that problem?

Here is an example:

The average of 3, 5, 6, and x is 6. What is x? Since we know that the average is 6, we figured it out backwards. There are four numbers here: 3, 5, 6, and x. The sum of these numbers divided by four is the average.

$$(3 + 5 + 6 + x) / 4 = 6$$

$$3 + 5 + 6 + x = 6 \times 4 = 24$$

$$x = 24 - 3 - 5 - 6$$

$$x = 10$$

We can then verify this by adding the values:

$$3 + 5 + 6 + 10 = 24$$

$$24 / 4 = 6$$

Now that we have looked at these examples, what about the average rate? This is often seen in examples that are worded as: Average A per B. Here is an example to help you understand average rate:

Frank packaged 17 boxes in 3 hours and then 37 boxes in 4 hours. What is his average box per hour rate?

Well, average box per hour rate = total boxes/total hours

= (17 + 37) / (3 + 4)

= 54/7

= 7.714 boxes per hour is his average.

Statistics and Probability

Once again, if you pay attention to sports, then you already have a handle on statistics, and probably a bit of a handle on probability.

With statistics and probability, we will deal with various terms like mean, mode, median, range, and standard deviation. Standard deviation is the measure of a set of numbers (how much they deviate from the mean or average). The greater the spread, the higher the standard deviation.

Thankfully, you never have to calculate standard deviation on the GMAT, so we will move on. However, it does help to know what standard deviation means.

Probability, as any gambler knows, is determined for a finite number of outcomes. Obviously, the higher the probability, the greater the possibility that a desirable or undesirable outcome will occur.

Let's look at an example.

We find probability by dividing the number of desired outcomes by the number of total possible outcomes:

$$P = D/T$$

John is reaching into a prize bin with 321 names on it, including seven names of people whom he knows. Therefore, what is the chance that John pulls out the name of someone he knows?

$$7 = D;\ 321 = T$$

$$P = 7 / 321$$

$$P = .022$$

Therefore, the probability of John selecting someone he knows is .022, or 2.2%

Of course, calculating this form of probability is easy. What is not so easy is calculating the probability of a certain outcome after multiple repetitions of the same or different experiment. Typically, you will find that these questions come in two different forms. One is where each event must occur in a set way, and another is where each event has different outcomes.

To determine the probability in multiple-event situations, we look at two things:

- Find out the probability of each event;
- Multiply the probabilities together.

Let's look at an example to understand this further:

There are 15 Canadians and 15 Russians in the NHL Entry Draft. What is the probability that the first two picks of the draft will both be Canadian?

Looking at the fractions of these two picks, we have 15 / 30 and 15 / 30, which can both be reduced to ½.

Once one draft pick is made, there is a 14 / 29 possibility that the next pick will be a Canadian player. Therefore, we multiply the two fractions:

$$(1 / 2) \times (14 / 29)$$

$$= 7 / 29$$

This then converts to .24 in decimal form.

As a result, the chance of two Canadian players being selected first and second in the draft is 24%.

The previous example calculated the probability that each individual event will occur a certain way. What about situations in which different outcomes may occur?

To calculate this, we must determine the total number of possible outcomes by figuring out the number of possible outcomes for each individual event and multiplying those together. For example:

Audy sees four doors. Behind some is money, behind others is nothing. What are the chances that Audy finds money behind three of the four doors?

Since each door has two possible outcomes, four tries have (2 x 2 x 2 x 2) = 16 possible outcomes. We list the possible outcomes where three of the four doors have money behind them.

$ = Money, E = Nothing

$ $ $ E $ E $ $ $ $ $ $

$ $ E $ E $ $ $

Now we know that there are five outcomes where money is behind three of the four doors; therefore, the number of possible desired outcomes is 5 and the number of possible total outcomes is 16. Using what we learned a few pages back, we have the following:

5 / 16

= .3125

= 31.25%

11

Ratios

What are ratios? Anyone… Anyone?

Well, they are the comparison of two quantities by division. That's it!

So, on to the next section!

Actually, there is a bit more to know about ratios than just that.

Typically, ratios can be written in two ways: as a fraction (y / z) and with a colon (y:z). You can also say "the ratio of y to z" if you want.

Usually, ratios are expressed as y / z.

Whenever you are dealing with ratios, it is always best to reduce them to their lowest terms.

Craig is 26, Layla is 22.

The ratio of Craig's age to Layla's age is 26 / 22 (26 to 22).

Therefore the lowest terms are 13 / 11.

Ratios, which are worded in the way we have seen, "y to z," should be turned into this format:

The ratio of 17 to 22 is 17 / 22.

When working with ratios, we often hear the word "proportion," which is simply an equation in which two ratios are equal to one another.

Ratios are two pieces, parts, and wholes, where the whole is the entire set and the part is the portion we are taking out.

Describing a ratio is then worded as "what fraction of the whole is this part?"

Or, to more easily understand this, let's look at this example:

Out of 37 players on the British Lions team, 12 are from Ireland.

So, the whole is 37, and the part is 12.

Therefore, the question can now be worded as:

What fraction of the British Lions team is from Ireland?

12 / 37

= 32.4 percent

Knowing what we do about ratios, let's move on to part ratios and whole ratios. A ratio can either compare a part to a part or a part to a whole.

The ratio of trucks to cars is 2:7. As a result, what fraction of the total cars and trucks is trucks?

By adding 2 and 7, we know that for every 9 vehicles, 2 are trucks, which means that the fraction or ratio of trucks to total cars and trucks is:

2 /(2 + 7)

2 / 9

Ratios with more than two terms are usually ratios of various parts, and usually these parts equal the whole, which allows us to find the part : whole ratio.

The ratio of trucks to cars to SUVs is: 2:7:3

What ratios can be determined here?

Ratio of trucks = 2 / (2+7+3)

Ratio of trucks = 2 / 12 = 1 / 6

Ratio of cars = 7 / 12

Ratio of SUVs = 3 / 12 = 1 / 4

Ratio of SUVs to cars and trucks = 3:9

Ratio of trucks to cars: 2:7

Ratio of cars to trucks and SUVs = 7:5

As we have seen above, ratios are always reduced to their simplest form, which can cause some confusion. Just because the ratio of trucks to total vehicles is 2:12, this does not mean that only two trucks were sold. The actual ratio may be much higher, like 20:120.

By knowing the actual number of total vehicles, we cannot know the actual values of the ratio.

Let's move on to rates. A rate is a ratio that compares two different types of quantities, often seen in the example of miles per hour:

Henry drove 126 miles in four hours. His average rate is:

126 / 4 = 31.5 miles per hour

That is all there is to rates. They are more or less the same as averages.

12

PERCENTAGES

Probably one of the most common forms of math relationships is percentages. We all know what percentages are and usually deal with them on a regular basis. As a result, it is highly likely that you will find percent questions on the GMAT.

Percentages are very easy to figure out from their decimal or fraction form:

23 / 100 = .23 = 23%

To turn a fraction into a decimal, all we do is divide the numerator by the denominator. To get our percentage, we simply multiply our decimal form by 100:

.23 x 100 = 23%

The same is true when we want to move backwards from a percentage to decimal form to fraction form:

16 divided by 100 = .16 = 16 / 100 = 4 / 25

Now that we have gone over that incredibly easy piece of information dealing with percentages, we move on to problems involving percents.

Most of these problems will come in the form, “What is (percent) of (variable)?” Or, put in a way similar to what we covered with ratios: percent x whole = part.

What is 32% of 183?

.32 x 183 = 58.56

We can do the reverse when we want to figure out a question worded like this: “13 is 37.1 percent of what number?” To determine this, we use the format of whole = part / percent:

X = 13 / 37.1%

X = 35

Of course, this can be avoided if you have certain percentages in your question. For example, “40 is 50 percent of what number?” This is easy to answer because we know that 50 percent is half, so 40 x 2 = 80, which is the number we are looking for. This primarily works for 10, 25, 50, and 75 percent.

Now, if we have the whole and the part, how do we figure out the percentage? Easy! We just reorganize the previous formula to read % = part / whole.

22 is what percent of 293?

% = 22 / 293

= .075

% = .075 x 100

= 7.5%

Moving on now, let's review percent increases and decreases, along with combining percentages.

First, when you increase or decrease a percentage, be careful about the amount of the increase or decrease of the original whole, not the new figure.

If the price of a $30,000 car increases by 13 percent, what is the new price?

All we do is take the original price of $30,000 and multiply it by the percentage:

30,000 x .13 = 3900

This means that the increase was $3,900 and the new price is:

30,000 + 3,900 = 33,900

The new selling price is $33,900.

Combining percentages is simply taking one percent and applying it to another. Here is an example:

The price of a car is $20,000, but that was reduced recently by 17 percent, and then was reduced by another 8 percent. What is the final price?

So, if a price was reduced by 17 percent, then it is:

100 % – 17 % = 83% of what it once was.

The new price is then 20,000 x .83 = 16,600.

Now, we reduce that by 5%:

16,600 x .05 = 830

16,600 – 830 = 15,770

The final price is $15,770.

An important point should be made here. You have to reduce the price from the same number; you cannot simply add the percentages together. We will use the same variables in this question to see the incorrect results that this creates:

17% + 5% = 22%

20,000 x .22 = 4,400

20,000 – 4,400 = 15,600

The value is close, but close only counts in horseshoes, and on your GMAT, it does not count at all.

13

Exponentiation

When we think of zy^x, z is the coefficient, y is the base and x is the exponent. The exponent is the number of times the base of something is multiplied by itself.

$$2^2 = 2 \times 2 = 4$$

$$2^4 = 2 \times 2 \times 2 \times 2 = 16$$

In terms of multiplying and dividing, these are done in generally the same way as we have seen over the course of this book. Here is an example:

$$2^3 \times 2^4 = (2 \times 2 \times 2) \times (2 \times 2 \times 2 \times 2)$$

$$= 8 \times 16$$

$$= 128$$

$$2^4 / 2^3 = (2 \times 2 \times 2 \times 2) / (2 \times 2 \times 2)$$

$$= 16 / 8$$

$$= 2$$

Sometimes, you may have to raise your exponent to another exponent, but this can easily be done as well:

$$(4^2)^3 = (4 \times 4)^3$$

$$16^3 = 16 \times 16 \times 16$$

$$= 4096$$

What about negative exponents? Well, they aren't fun but you have to learn about them. In this case, a negative exponent means that a reciprocal is used. To find the solution, all we have to do is take the reciprocal of the base and change the sign of the exponent.

$$2^{-4} = (1 / 2)^4$$

$$= 1 / 2^4$$

$$= 1 / (2 \times 2 \times 2 \times 2)$$

$$= 1 / 16$$

That is about all there is to know about calculating the power of something. You won't have many questions such as these on your GMAT, but you'll see a few so be sure you know how to do them.

14

ALGEBRA

So it has come to this. We all remember algebra from high school math, and most likely, we all hated doing it. Now here you are, ready to plunge into algebra again for the GMAT.

Well, don't worry because while algebra is a part of the GMAT, it is a small part, and only makes up 20% of the entire math section.

We can skip over this and forget about algebra altogether, or we can plunge headlong into it and get it over with. So, let's go.

Terminology

When we say *term*, we are referring to the numerical constant, or the product of a numerical constant, plus one or more variables. Terms come in many different formats, such as: 7x, 21y, and 3x/y.

Expressions, like an algebraic expression, are combinations of a variety of terms. These expressions are separated by a + or – sign, for example:

$$7x + 21y - 3x/y$$

Substitution is very important in algebra, and it involves a method that is used to evaluate the expression.

For example:

Evaluate $7x + 21y$ if $x = 2$ and $y = 1$

This means the numbers will be substituted into the expression as:

$$(7 \times 2) + (21 \times 1)$$

$$= 14 + 21$$

$$= 35$$

We previously discussed the various laws of operations, and those same laws apply to polynomial expressions in algebra.

These laws include the commutative law, the associative law, and at times both laws. The distributive law is also found in algebraic expressions.

Factoring Expressions

When you factor a polynomial expression, you are expressing it as the product of two or more simpler expressions.

The common monomial factor is common to every term in the polynomial and can be factored out using the distributive law.

The difference of two perfect squares can be factored into the product of:

$$b^2 - c^2 = (b - c)(b + c)$$

Polynomials using the expression $a^2 + 2ab + b^2$ are equivalent to the square of a binomial.

$$(a + b)^2 = a^2 + 2ab + b^2$$

Polynomials of the form $a^2 - 2ab + b^2$ are equivalent to the square of a binomial, where the binomial is the difference between the two terms:

$$(a - b)^2 = a^2 - 2ab + b^2$$

Polynomials of the form $x^2 + bx + c$ can always be factored into a product of two binomials. More specifically:

$$(x + m)(x + n) = x^2 + (m+n)x + mn$$

This may seem like a lot to take in, but don't worry, you will get the hang of it – and algebra is only a small portion of the test.

15

Word Problems

Word problems will test what you learned in algebra, arithmetic, and even geometry from your school years. All they do is ask the same questions in a different way. Look at this example to understand how:

In Algebra Form: $3x + 2 = y$

In Word Problem Form: If the number of cars on the lot tripled, the car lot would have only 2 less than the lot next door.

In this case, the number of cars on the lot is x, and the lot next door is y.

If $x = 23$ cars then: $3(23) + 2 = y$

The number of cars (y) on the other lot is 71.

The key to understanding word problems is to convert what they are saying in English into the universal language of mathematics. This is sometimes easier said than done.

Let's do some simple math to ease back into the concept of word problems. We will cover addition, multiplication, subtraction, and division in the next four examples.

If Jim bought eight apples for \$.29 each and four pears for \$.79 each, how much did he pay in total?

$$(8 \times .29) + (4 \times .79)$$

$$= 2.32 + 3.16$$

$$= 5.48$$

If there are 72 people in the room and 27 are adult men and 33 are children, how many women are there in the room?

$$72 - 27 - 33$$

$$= 45 - 33$$

$$= 12$$

If you buy one television for \$3,300, then how many will 9 cost you?

$$3{,}300 \times 9$$

$$= \$29{,}700$$

If Jason bought eight apples for \$3.72, how much is each apple?

$$3.72 / 8$$

$$= 47 \text{ cents}$$

Right there, we can see quickly and easily what we are dealing with – all based on the information in the word problems. Most simple mathematical word problems follow this method.

Since we just covered algebra, it's now time to put algebra into word problems. This may help you understand the problem much better. Let's look at an example to see how algebra fits into word problems.

Frank weighs the sum of Jim's weight multiplied by two, and Mary's weight multiplied by three. This can be shown as:

$$F = 2J + 3M$$

Of course, we need more information to answer this question. If we know that J = 120 and M = 97, then we can do more math:

$$F = 2(120) + 3(97)$$

$$F = 240 + 291$$

$$F = 531$$

So, Frank weights 531 pounds and should start looking into joining a gym.

That's it for the basics of word problems. In the next section, we will move on to more complex problems.

16

Word Problems with Percents, Ratios, and Rates

Surprisingly, many word problems relate to percentages. And, most percentage problems actually come in word form. Since we already know how percentages work, we will delve right into these word problems. Let's review a few examples.

Chris makes 17% off each television and 23% off each DVD player that he sells. In one day, he sold four televisions each worth $988, and two DVD players each worth $127. How much did he make on that day?

$$4 \times (988 \times .17) + 2 \times (127 \times .23)$$

$$= 4 \times 167.96 + 2 \times 29.21$$

$$= 730.26$$

Chris made $730.26

Brandon and Laura sell jeans on their Web site. One pair costs $29.99. If you buy ten pairs, then you get 10% off. If you buy 100 pairs, then you get 30% off. How much do Brandon and Laura make if they sell 10 pairs to one customer and 100 pairs to another customer?

$$\text{Difference} = ((29.99 \times 10) \times .10) + ((29.99 \times 100) \times .3))$$

We have to remember to use the Law of Operations here.

$$\text{Difference} = (299.90 \times .10) + (2999 \times .3)$$

$$\text{Difference} = 29.99 + 899.7 = 929.69$$

$$\text{Profit} = (299.90 + 2999) - 929.69$$

$$\text{Profit} = 3298.9 - 929.69 = 2369.21$$

Other common word problems use ratios and rates. We have already reviewed ratios and rates, so let's move on to the examples.

There are five oranges in a bag, along with three apples and two plums. What is the ratio of apples to oranges and plums to apples?

Oranges = 5

Apples = 3

Plums = 2

Apples to Oranges: 3:5

Plums to Apples: 2:3

Taking the above into consideration, what is the ratio of oranges to total fruit?

Total fruit = 5 + 3 + 2 = 10

Oranges to Total Fruit: 5:10 = 1:2

Rates. If Jim jogs 12 miles in five hours, what is his average speed?

Speed = 12 / 5

Speed = 2.4 miles per hour

Using the data from the above question, if Jim continues jogging for another three and a half hours, how much distance will he cover?

Distance = rate x time

Distance = 2.4 x 3.5

Distance = 8.4 miles

That is about all there is for ratios, percentages, and rates in word problems. Having covered these topics in arithmetic form makes things much easier when you begin to tackle the word problems.

17

Geometry

Geometry on the GMAT is very basic and the questions relate just to lines, triangles, circles, and other relevant concepts. So you only need to know a few fundamental definitions and formulas.

Diagrams are a big part of the geometry portion of the exam, and here are a few things to keep in mind when dealing with diagrams.

All diagrams on the GMAT are to scale, unless otherwise noted by the question. This means that you can eliminate a lot of choices simply by looking at the diagram and estimating what you see in terms of length.

We will begin by reviewing lines and angles.

As we know, a line is a one-dimensional object. It has no width, and is infinitely long. A line segment is part of a straight line, and has two endpoints. Typically, a line is named for its end points: AB. The midpoint of the line is the point on the line segment that divides the line in two equal parts.

In the above example, A and B are the endpoints. M, the midpoint, is in the exact middle of line segment AB.

If we know that the distance between AM is 6, then the distance between MB is also 6. This means that the total distance of line AB is 12.

We know that an angle is formed whenever two lines, or line segments, intersect at a certain point. This point is the vertex of the angle, and the angle is measured in degrees.

There are four common types of angles.

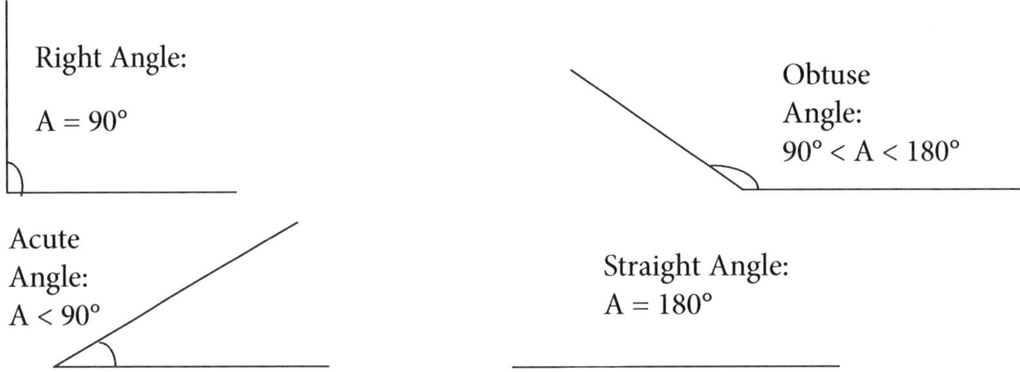

A right angle is exactly 90 degrees. An acute angle is less than 90 degrees, while an obtuse angle is greater than 90 degrees but less than 180 degrees. A straight angle is 180 degrees.

Lines are perpendicular if they are at 90-degree angles to each other.

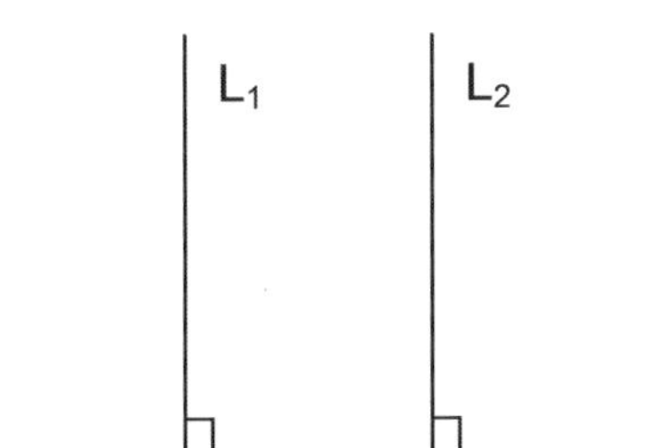

When two angles added together measure 180 degrees, then the lines that make up the angles are called supplementary. If the angles measure 90 degrees, the corresponding lines are complimentary.

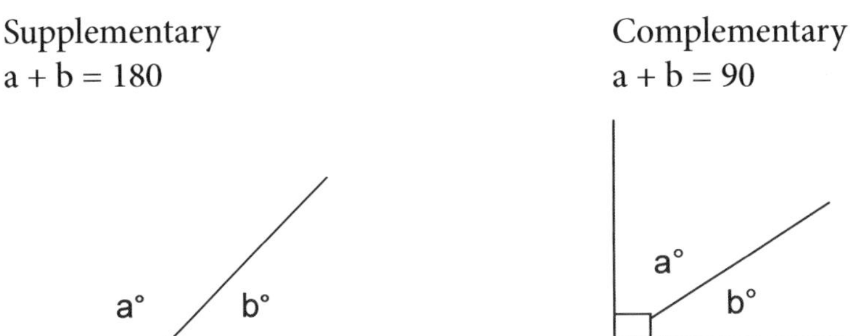

As can be seen from the examples above, when a line goes through an angle, it splits it into two smaller angles. If the split is equal, then the line is said to bisect an angle. A line that splits a 90-degree angle into two 45-degree angles is known as bisecting that angle.

Two intersecting lines create vertical angles, which are the opposite angles formed at the point of intersection. In the example below, w and y are vertical angles, as are x and z.

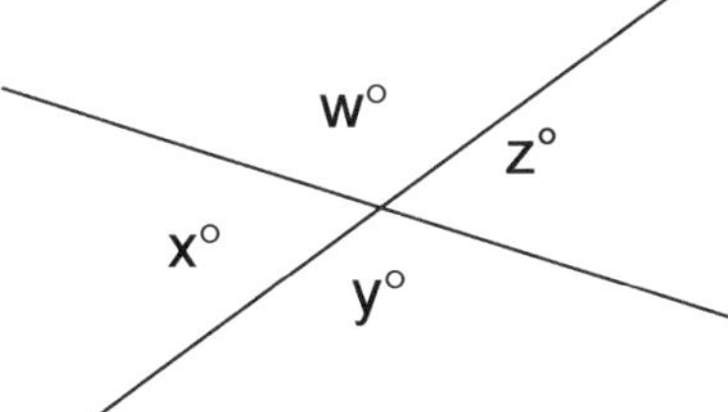

In the example above, $x = z$ and $w = y$; therefore:

$$w + x = y + z = w + z = x + y = 180.$$

If two parallel lines are intersected by a third line, which is called a transversal, the two parallel lines will intersect that third line at the same angle, as can be seen below.

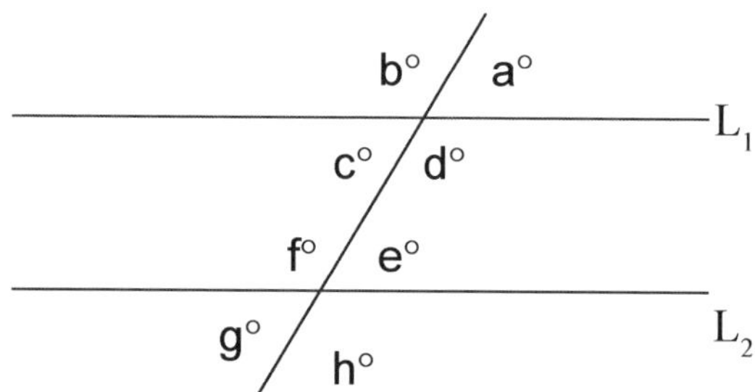

In the example above, we see that *a* and *e* are equal to each other. Also, since $a = c$ and $e = g$, then $a = c = e = g$ while $b = d = f = h$.

The next concept that we will look at here is slope. When we talk about slope, we are talking about how steeply a line goes up or down. If a line gets higher as you move to the right, then the slope is positive. Conversely, if a line gets lower as it goes to the right, then it has a negative slope.

It is actually quite easy to find the slope of a line using the equation:

Slope = rise / run

The rise is the difference between the y-coordinate values of the two points on the line, while the run is the difference between the x-coordinates on the lines. Let's look at an example below.

What is the slope of a line with two end points at (2, 1) and (3, 6)?

Slope = change in y / change in x

Slope = (6-1)/(3-2)

Slope = 5 / 1

Therefore, the slope is 5

However, not all of the questions will give you the coordinates of a line, and you will have to figure out the slope using nothing but an equation. Thankfully, that is not hard to do. All that we have to do is turn the equation into $y = mx + b$, where m is the slope of the line and b is the y-intercept.

18

TRIANGLES

We all know what a triangle is and how it looks, but there are a few more things we need to learn about triangles for the GMAT.

First, remember the rule that helps when figuring out the angles of a triangle: The sum of the interior angles of any triangle is 180 degrees. Each interior angle in a triangle is supplementary to an adjacent exterior angle. The degrees of the exterior angle are then equal to the sum of the measures of the two non-adjacent, interior angles.

Let's look at an example to help clear this up.

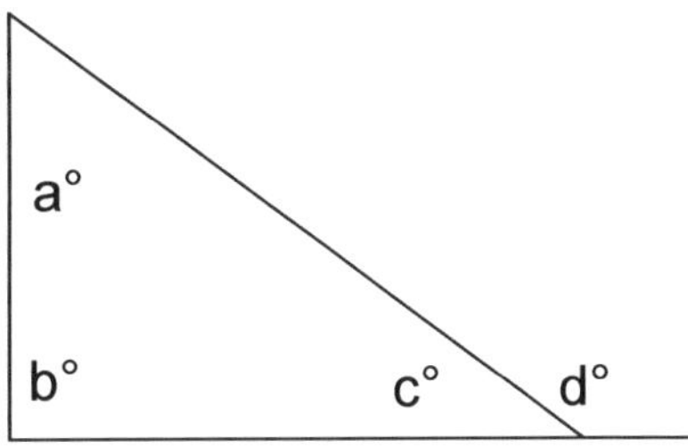

In this figure, the interior angles are a, b, and c, while d is the exterior angle. Looking at the three interior angles, a + b + c = 180 degrees, and since d is supplemental to c,

$d + c = 180$. Therefore, $d + c = a + b + c$ and $d = a + b$. That means that d is equal to the sum of the two remote angles in the triangle: a and b.

Let's look at a brief equation for this:

If $a = 45$ and $b = 90$, then $45 + 90 = d$, and

$d = 135$. Therefore the angle is 135°.

The altitude of a triangle is the distance between the vertex and the side opposite the vertex. This can be inside, or even outside, the triangle.

Let's look at two examples of the triangle vertex, inside and outside.

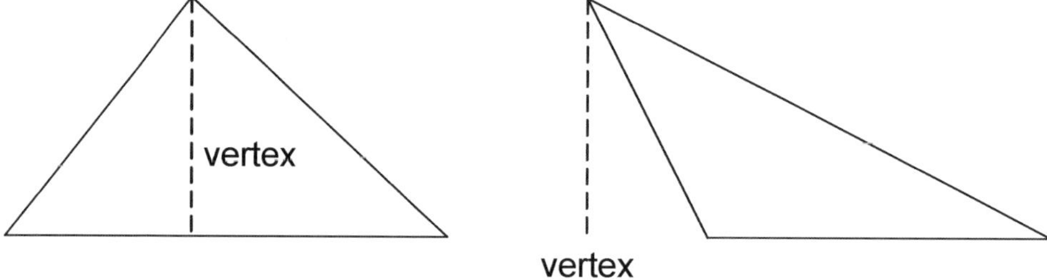

The sides of a triangle are very important. They allow us to figure out the area of the triangle when we do not have all of the information at our disposal. The length of each side of a triangle is less than the sum of the lengths of the other two sides, and greater than the positive difference of the lengths of the other two sides. This can be seen in the following equations:

$b + c > a > b - c$

$a + b > c > a - b$

$a + c > b > a - c$

Knowing this, we can begin to figure out the area of a triangle.

The area of a triangle can be figured out with the following formula:

$A = ½(b \times h)$

where A = area, b = base and h = height.

If a triangle has a base length of 6 and an altitude (vertex) height of 3, then we have an area as follows:

$A = ½(6 \times 3)$

$A = ½ \times 18$

$A = 9$

If we are dealing with a right angle triangle, then we can use the following formula to calculate the area:

$A = 1/2L_1 \times L_2$

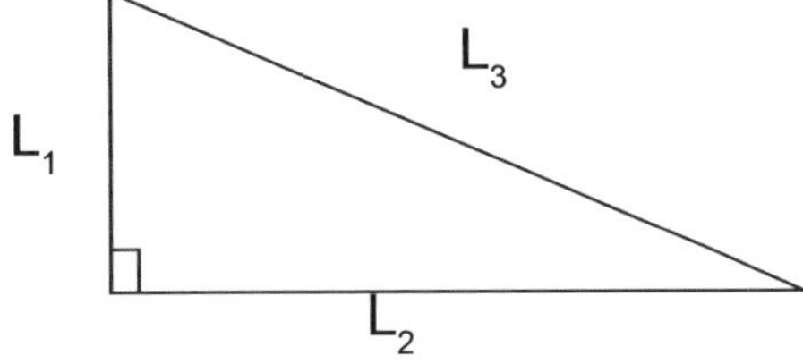

L_1 and L_2 are always the legs that come out from the right angle. If their value is 9 and 21, respectively, then we can figure out the area of the triangle.

$A = ½(6) \times 21$

$A = 3 \times 21$

A = 63

When perimeter is talked about in terms of triangles, it means the distance around the triangle. This means that the perimeter is equal to the sum of the lengths of the sides.

Here is an example:

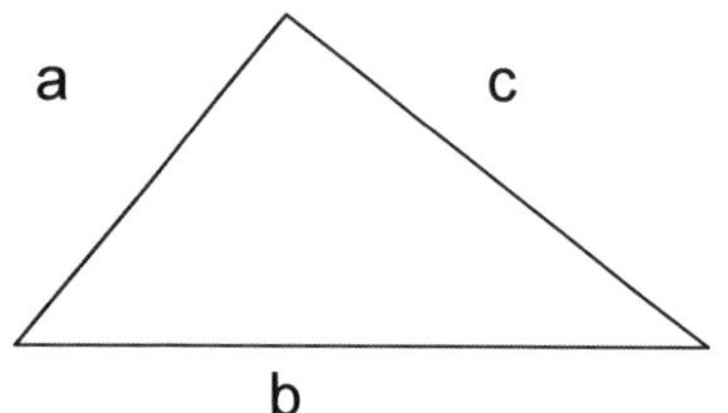

a = 5

b = 13

c = 12

P = 5 + 13 + 12

P = 30

We already know about right triangles, but what about the other two types of triangles?

An isosceles triangle is a triangle with two sides of equal length, called the legs, while the third side is the base. As a result of the legs being the same length, the two legs on opposite sides of each other have the same angle.

In this triangle, b = c.

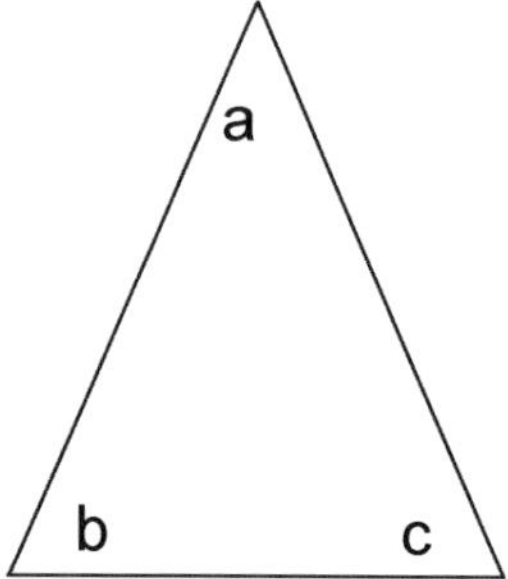

The other type of triangle is the equilateral triangle. These triangles have three sides of equal length, and three 60-degree angles.

Right angles are the most recognizable triangles in geometry. The longest side of the right angle triangle is called the hypotenuse, while the other two sides are the legs, as mentioned in the previous example .

To calculate the area of a triangle, we can use one of the most famous mathematical equations in history: the Pythagorean Theorem.

This theorem dictates that the square of the hypotenuse is equal to the sum of the squares of the other two sides. Expressed as an equation, it reads:

$a^2 = b^2 + c^2$

Let's look at an example of this for a better understanding of how the equation is used.

What is the length of the hypotenuse if the legs are of lengths 11 and 12?

$a^2 = 11^2 + 12^2$

$a^2 = 121 + 144$

$a^2 = 265$

$a = 16.27$

For that GMAT, that is about all we need to know about triangles. It is important to remember the differences between triangles, as well as how to find their areas and perimeters.

Only a few more sections and we will be done with geometry!

19

Polygons and Quadrilaterals

Not everyone knows what polygons or quadrilaterals are, but chances are good that they have seen them on a regular basis in their day-to-day lives.

A polygon is a closed figure with straight-line segments for sides. This means that the perimeter of a polygon is the sum of the lengths of its sides.

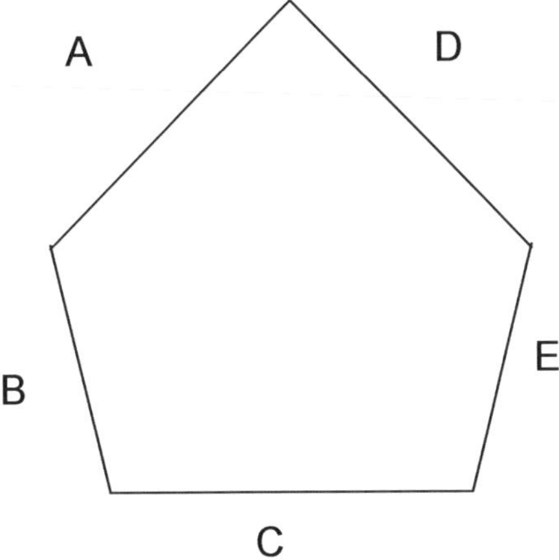

In the example above, we can calculate the perimeter as follows:

$$A + B + C + D + E$$

So, if B = E, A = D, and B = 2, A = 3 and C = 4, then the total perimeter is:

$$3 + 2 + 4 + 3 + 2 = 14$$

The diagonal of the polygon is a line segment connected to two nonadjacent vertices. When you hear the term "regular polygon," it means that the polygon has sides of equal length and interior angles of equal measure.

Polygons have different names, depending on the number of sides that they have. If it has three sides, it is called a triangle. If it has four sides, it is a quadrilateral. If it has five sides, it is a pentagon. If it has six sides, it is a hexagon. Triangles and quadrilaterals appear most frequently on the GMAT.

The interior and exterior angles of a polygon can easily be found by simply dividing the polygon into triangles. See below for an example:

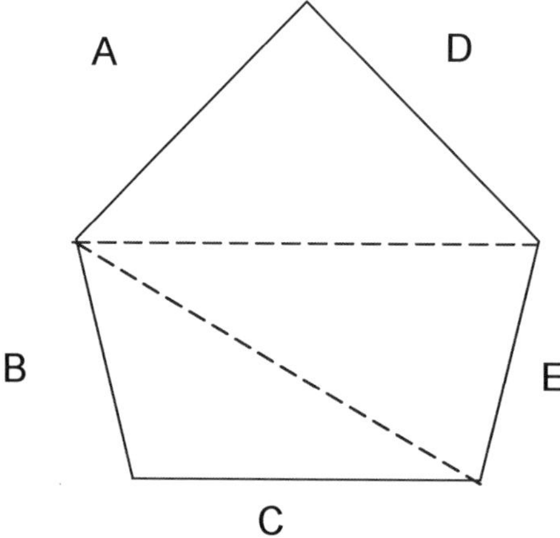

From the previous chapter, we already know that the sum of the interior angles of a triangle is 180 degrees. Since there are three triangles whose interior angles add up to 180 degrees, the sum of the interior angles in the polygon is 3 x 180 degrees, or 540 degrees.

Let's look at another example:

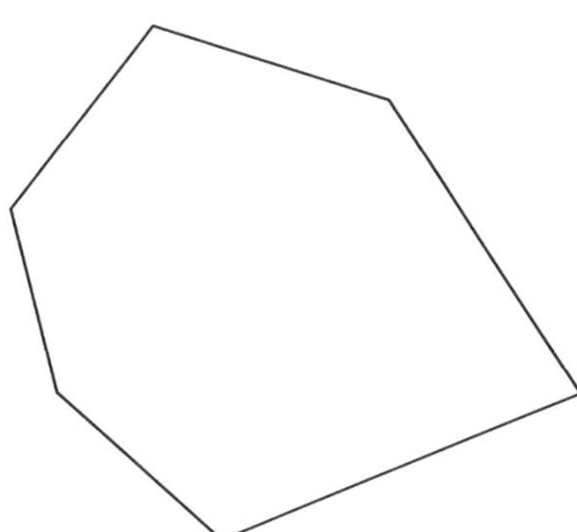

In the example above, what is the sum of the angles if the polygon is divided into three sections with three interior lines?

Dividing the polygon creates four triangles. Therefore, the total sum of the angles is 180 x 4 = 720 degrees.

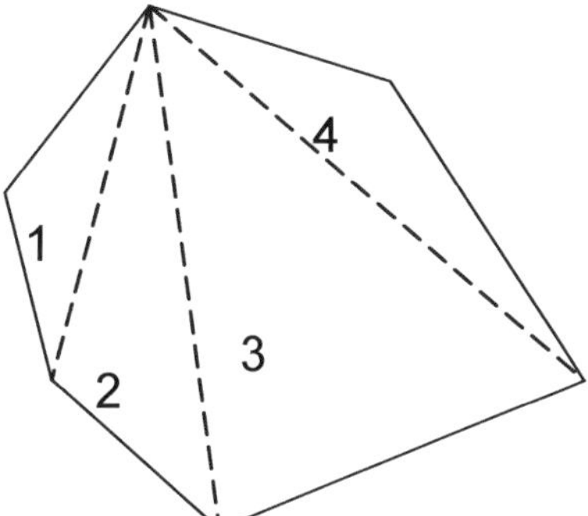

Quadrilaterals are the most important aspect of geometry that appears on the GMAT, since they are by far the most frequently encountered concept on the test. We will cover them in-depth here.

A quadrilateral, as we mentioned above, is a four-sided polygon, where the sum of the interior angles equals 360 degrees in total.

The two most common forms of quadrilaterals are squares and rectangles. A rectangle is a quadrilateral with four equal right angles, with the opposite sides of the rectangles equal in length. A square is a rectangle of four equal sides and angles.

Calculating the area of quadrilaterals, like squares and rectangles, is easy. To find the area of a rectangle, simply multiply the length of the rectangle by the width ($A = l \times w$), while the area of a square is its side squared, since all sides are of equal length ($A = s^2$). Let's look at a few examples:

What is the area of this rectangle?

$A = l \times w$

$A = 19 \times 14$

$A = 266$

What is the area of this square?

$A = s^2$

$A = 13^2$

$A = 169$

20

Circles

Do we all know what a circle is? Good, then let's move on to the next section.

As nice as it would be to skip this section, many of the questions that you will see related to geometry have to do with circles. It is important that we cover circles here. Thankfully, circles are pretty easy to understand.

Defining a circle is a bit harder than simply looking at it. In layman's terms, if all points on a plane from a certain point are of the same distance, then you have a circle. This point is the center of the circle, and all circles are labeled for their center point. The diameter of a circle is a line that connects two points of a circle and passes through the center point. The radius is a line segment from the center to the edge of the circle and is always one-half the length of the diameter.

Central angles are formed by the radii coming out from the center of the circle.

A tangent of a circle is a line that touches only one point on the circle and runs perpendicular to it.

Now we get to one of the most important pieces of information related to a circle: Pi. The circumference of a circle is the distance around a circle. Pi is the ratio of a circle's circumference to its diameter. The value of Pi is 3.1415926… and the decimal places never, ever end. In fact, Pi is the longest non-repeating number in the universe. Thankfully, you only need to remember it to two places, or 3.14. Since Pi is equal to the ratio of the circumference to the diameter, the formula to find the circumference is C = (pi)d or C = 2(pi)r.

Before moving on to arcs and areas, let's just draw a circle and figure out some of the stuff we have just talked about here.

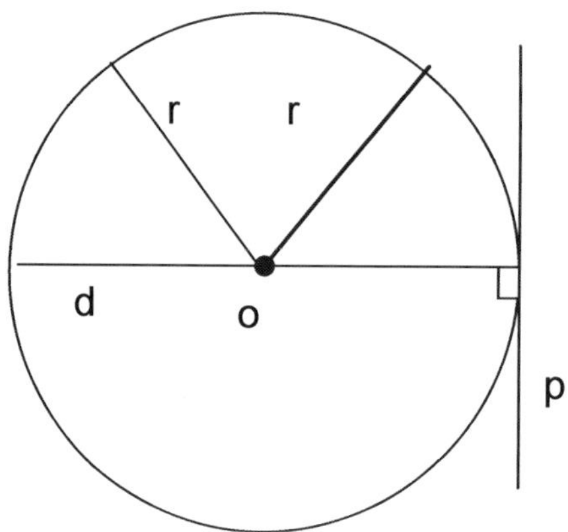

o = center of the circle

r = radius line

p = perpendicular line

d = diameter line

Now, the arc of a circle is the portion of the circumference of a circle. A major arc is an arc of a circle having measure greater than or equal to 180 degrees, while a minor arc is an arc of a circle having measure less than or equal to 180 degrees. If the arc is exactly half the circumference, then it is a semi-circle. Let's look at three examples.

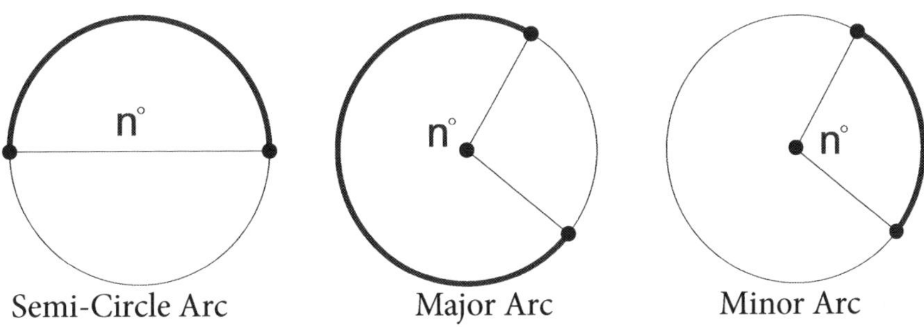

To find the length of the arc with a central point, we use the formula:

Arc length = (n / 360) x circumference

Let's look at an example.

What is the length of the arc XYZ?

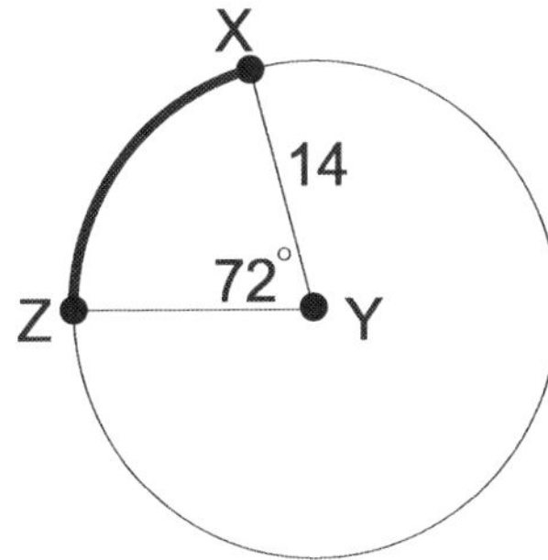

Since we know that the length of the radii is 14, we can figure out the circumference.

$$C = 2(pi)r$$

$$C = 2(3.14) \times 14$$

$$C = 6.28 \times 14$$

$$C = 87.92$$

We know the angle is 72 degrees, which means it is 72 out of 360 degrees or:

$$72 / 360 = 1 / 5$$

This means that the length of the arc is one-fifth the circumference or:

$$1/5 \times 87.92$$

The equation for the area of a circle also uses Pi in the formula Area = $(pi)r^2$. Let's find out the circumference and area of the circle below:

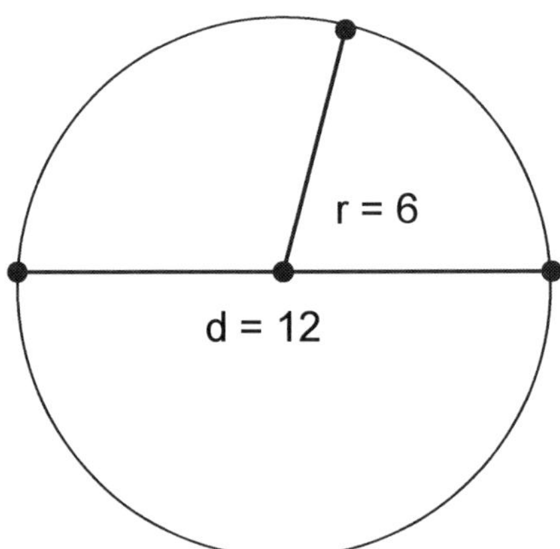

Since we know the diameter and the radii, it is easy to figure out the circumference and the area.

$$\text{Circumference} = \text{pi} \times d$$

$$C = 3.14 \times 12$$

$$C = 37.68$$

$$\text{Area} = \text{pi} \times r^2$$

$$A = 3.14 \times 6^2$$

$$A = 3.14 \times 36$$

$$A = 113.04$$

There we have it – the area and the circumference of the circle. Now it is time to move on.

21

Multiple Figures

One aspect of geometry that you may not be familiar with is the concept of multiple figures. You will probably see multiple figures on your test, albeit not many of them.

Multiple figures are combinations of shapes, and you may find that the hypotenuse of a triangle is the side of a rectangle. Since you will be required to find the area of a particular shape, you need an eye for shapes.

Let's look at a sample question for a better understanding of this.

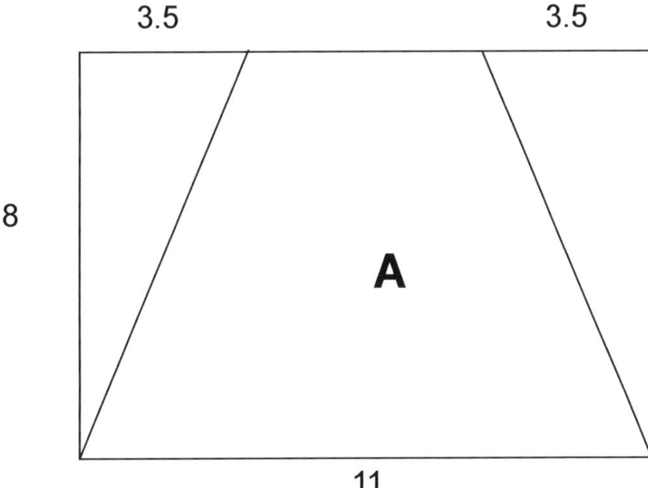

What is the perimeter of the polygon A?

To figure this out, we have to look at the shapes inside the rectangle. We can clearly see a right angle triangle.

Since we know that $a^2 = b^2 + c^2$, we can figure out one side of the polygon:

$$a^2 = 8^2 + 3.5^2$$

$$a^2 = 64 + 12.25$$

$$a^2 = 76.25$$

$$a= 8.73$$

Now we know that one side of the polygon is 8.73. Since the triangle on the other side is the same shape, this means that the three sides of the polygon are 8.73, 8.73, and 11. To figure out the top side of the polygon, we use simple math.

$$11 - 3.5 - 3.5 = 4$$

Now we have all sides of the polygon, so the perimeter is:

$$a + b + c + d = 4 + 8.5 + 8.5 + 11$$

$$= 32$$

Another type of multiple figure is an inscribed or circumscribed figure, which is a polygon inscribed with a circle, or circumscribed about the circle. Here are two examples of this:

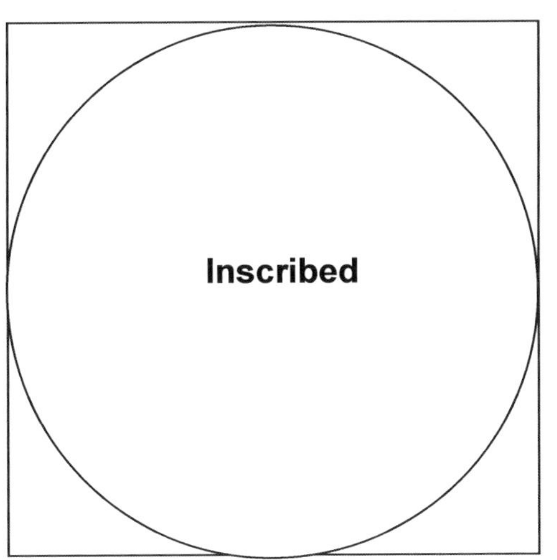

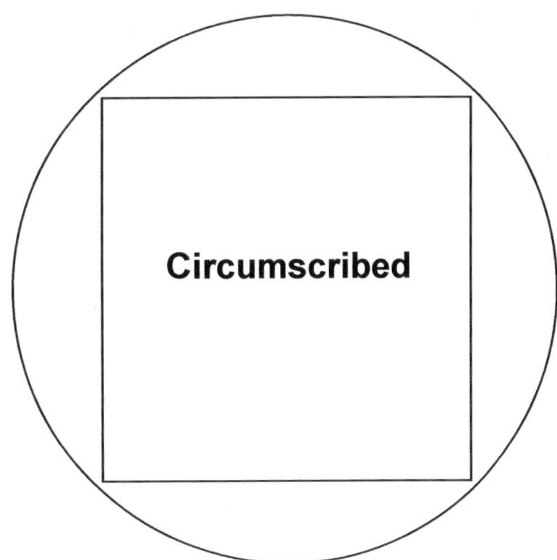

How do we figure out the perimeter of the square if we only know the circumference or diameter of the circle? Well, it is actually pretty easy. Let's look at an example.

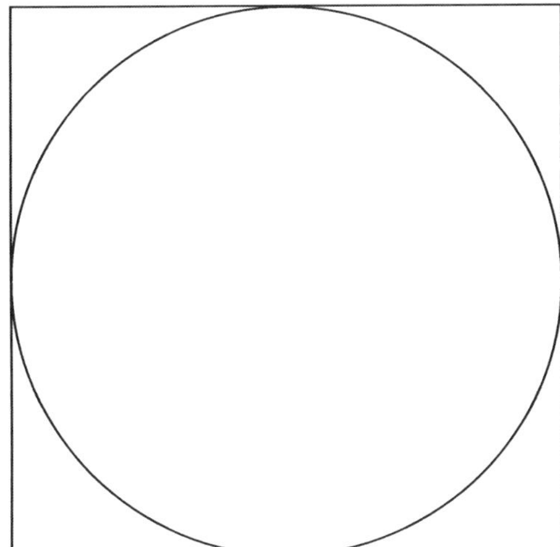

The area of the circle above is (pi)36. What is the perimeter of the square?

We know that the area of a circle is A = (pi)r^2. So if the area here is (pi)36, then we need the square of 36, which is 6.

Now that we know the radius, we can find the diameter, which is 6 x 2 = 12.

The diameter is 12, and since this is a square, all sides are equal. The diameter equals one side; therefore, the perimeter is:

$$12 + 12 + 12 + 12 = 48$$

We could also use the same information to find the area of the square:

Diameter of the circle = 12

Area of Square = 12^2

Therefore, the area of the square is 144.

Now, what about when we are dealing with a circumscribed figure? Let's do an example to figure it out.

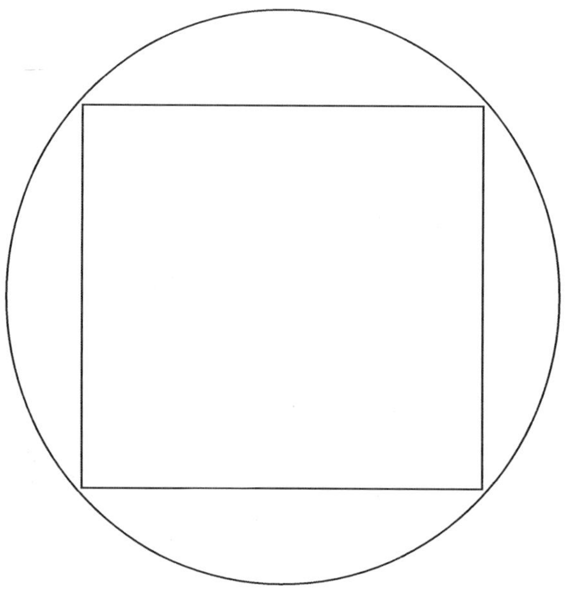

If the circumference of the square is 8, what is the area of the circle?

First we find the length of each side of the square: 8 / 4 = 2

Notice that the diagonal of the square is also the diameter of the circle. Our next step is to use the Pythagoras theorem to find the diagonal.

The diagonal is the square root of $(2^2 + 2^2)$ which equals $\sqrt{8}$.

Therefore the circle has a diameter of $\sqrt{8}$, and a radius of $(\sqrt{8} / 2)$

We get the area of the circle by using the equation:

$$\text{Area of circle} = (\sqrt{8} / 2)^2(\text{pi})$$

$$\text{Area} = 2(\text{pi})$$

The important thing to remember when you are working with multiple figures is to continue to view the object within the figure. This should help you begin to figure out how everything goes together. The above is a perfect example of this.

These are the primary shapes that you will have to deal with, and knowing your areas and perimeter formulas from previous chapters will help greatly in figuring out the answers to these questions.

22

Data Sufficiency

Now we come to a very unique part of the GMAT, the data sufficiency portion. These types of questions are only found on the GMAT, and about a third of the points available on the math section come from these questions. The rest of the points are from problem-solving questions, as we covered in previous sections.

With problem-solving questions, you are looking at the problem and finding the answer choice that best matches it. However, with data sufficiency, you don't care about the solution, you only have to answer the question if you are able to answer it with the information provided.

Throw away the calculator because data sufficiency questions require little or no use of it.

These types of questions will seem difficult at first, but as you move on, you will find that they get easier and easier.

All data sufficiency questions come in a similar format. You are given a question stem followed by two statements that, together or apart, may or may not answer the question in the passage. You have to choose one of the five options.

In the data sufficiency portion, you get a question followed by two statements that contain data. You then choose the correct answer based on the data in the statement, what you know, and common sense. Here is how the answers look:

1. Statement 1 alone is sufficient but statement 2 alone is not sufficient to answer the question asked.
2. Statement 2 alone is sufficient but statement 1 alone is not sufficient to answer the question asked.
3. Both statements 1 and 2 together are sufficient to answer the question but neither statement is sufficient alone.
4. Each statement alone is sufficient to answer the question.
5. Statements 1 and 2 are not sufficient to answer the question asked and additional data is needed to answer the statements.

You can use this effective method to try to answer data sufficiency questions when you come to them. It is an easy, step-by-step process.

1. Look at the question. This may seem self-explanatory, but the number of people who do not look at the questions when trying to answer them is surprising. You need to be able to decipher the question quickly, and then consider the information you may need to answer it properly. Do not be afraid to ask yourself questions like:
    i. What is the focus?

ii. Does it require a formula calculation?

iii. What are the variables?

iv. Do I have all of the values?

2. Next, as we have done with the reading part of the exam, we have to split everything up and look at it separately. Look at everything and try and determine again what you may need to answer it. You will want to go over the questions twice before moving on.

3. Look at the statements and make sure that you understand them. Focus on them and think about what you just read in the passage. By this time, you should be able to focus on what answers can remain and what answers you can eliminate. You can then begin to answer the question.

4. The last step is to answer the question to the best of your ability. Remember, it is better to get it wrong than skip it, so be sure to answer it.

That is about all there is to data sufficiency questions. For questions that make up a third of your math grade, they are pretty straightforward. Of course, don't worry, we aren't going to throw you to the wolves yet. We will look at a couple of questions here before moving on to the practice section.

Let's begin with a couple of questions to show you how it is all done. Don't worry, it is relatively easy once you get the hang of it.

What is the value of W if W and Z are two different integers and their sum in the equation W x Z = 60? You are also given the following statements:

1) W is an odd integer; and

2) W > Z.

The correct answer in this choice is 5, which is *The value of W cannot be determined from the information provided.* That is all well and good, but why is that the right answer?

We were given enough information to know that the two variables added together is 60. By looking at simple multiplication, we can determine that the following numbers conform to this:

1 x 60

2 x 30

4 x 15

3 x 20

5 x 12

6 x 10

Their negative values also conform (–1 x –60, etc).

We know that W is odd because of the statement, and that means W can be 1, 3, or 5, along with –1, –3, or –5. As a result, we cannot determine which of these will answer the question. From that data alone, we know that the first statement is automatically eliminated.

Also, since W has more than one value, we cannot use statement 2, which will not allow us to find the value of W.

Since we cannot get the value of W, the next two statements are also eliminated because they do not provide sufficient data to answer any of the questions. This is why the last statement is correct, because with statements 1 and 2 together, we are not able to answer the question and we need more information to do so.

How was that? Let's try one more before moving onto the practice section.

How is Francis related to Jessica?

1. Joseph, the husband of Francis' only sister Samantha, does not have siblings.
2. Jessica is Joseph's brother in law's wife.

Looking at the five answers, we can determine that answer 3 is the best choice for this question, which is *Both statements are required to answer the given question.*

We know from statement 1 that Joseph has no siblings and that he is the husband of Frances' sister, Samantha. This statement does not give us enough information, which eliminates answer 1 and answer 4.

The second statement tells us that Jessica is Joseph's brother-in-law's wife. This means that there is a relationship between Jessica and Joseph. This, however, does not answer how Francis is related to Jessica. Therefore, statement 3 is needed because we have the information to answer the question, but we need both statements together to do so.

Things to Remember...

Know that you do NOT need to know the solutions to the questions; you just need to know whether you can answer the question with the given information. Most data sufficiency questions do not require mathematical calculations and you can usually answer them faster than problem-solving questions. You need some practice to become familiar with data sufficiency questions because they are quite different. But once you are familiar with them, you'll find them easier than a lot of the problem-solving questions.

Here's how I answer data sufficiency questions:

1. Read the question quickly and decide what information is required to solve it. How many variables are in the equation? How many of them are unknown? Think before you look at the two statements, as this will help you quickly decide how relevant they are.

2. Read the two statements carefully and independently. Keep in mind that the information contained in each statement is unique and does not involve the other statement. Do not mix them up!

3. If both statements are insufficient individually to solve the question, look at them together and see if the information contained in both statements, taken together, is sufficient to solve the problem.

4. Finally, do NOT try to solve the question! As soon as you know whether the question can be solved, move on the next question and don't waste your time doing calculations.

5. For questions on number properties and algebra, you can come up with numbers and assign them to the variables and unknowns in the questions/statements to help you understand them better.

23

Analytical Writing

Despite the difficulty of critical reasoning, the headache of algebra, and the sheer confusion of data sufficiency, nothing strikes fear into the hearts of GMAT test takers like the analytical writing section.

It is easy to see why this section presents a problem for many. The first thing that you have to do on the GMAT is sit down and write two essays in 60 minutes. Most people don't write that much in 60 days, let alone 60 minutes.

On top of that, you will have no idea what the topic is that you are writing about. Of course, that does not mean that you can't look at the GMAC Web site to determine the current list of topics for the exam. This is not cheating. It is staying ahead of the game. See www.mba.com/mba/TaketheGMAT and www.mba.com/mba/thegmat/teststructureandoverview/analyticalwritingassessmentsection for more information.

Many people often wonder why applicants to business school need to be tested on their essay-writing skills. It is common knowledge that a person's success in business is related more to his or her verbal than written skills.

Plus, a lot of the people who take the GMAT are from overseas and their language, sentence structure, and grammar is very different from English, putting them at a disadvantage on this part of the exam.

We mentioned before that most schools don't even pay attention to the analytical portion of your test, and this is true. However, some do and it is better that you do well on it than poorly. You don't want to be rejected by the school of your choice simply because you slacked on the analytical writing portion of the GMAT.

This book is here to help you with learning how to pass the GMAT, and that is what we are going to do. We can't write the essay for you, but we can explain aspects about the essays that you will write and what you need to remember.

An "E-rater" or computer "bot" grading program that scans essays evaluates your essay. If the score from both the GMAT essay grader and the E-rater are in agreement, then that's the grade your essay will receive. If they disagree, then a second GMAT grader will grade your essay. The people who grade your essay vary, but initially they are part-time employees from the testing company, and are usually from graduate school programs.

How Much Time?

One common question is how much time graders spend on your essay. The truth is that they spend about two minutes each on one essay. They have to grade a lot of essays and they can't spend too much time on yours. The best that you can hope for here is a quick skim by the graders.

The computer grader takes even less time to grade your essay. All it does is compare your essay to other essays on the same topic. This means that if you are original in your methods and points, the computer won't be able to pick this out and you may actually be penalized.

The Best Piece of Advice

What do the graders look at the most when grading your essay? Is it your grammar? Your vocabulary? Your ideas?

Nope. It's the length of your essay.

If you want to do well on the essay portion of the exam, make sure that you write as much as you possibly can. Your essay should contain at least four paragraphs.

There. You just aced the essay portion of the GMAT.

Actually, it's not that easy but you would be surprised by how much length-of-essay factors into your grade.

The Principles

Prepare for a test when you don't know that the topic can be difficult. However, we have a few hints to help you prepare so that when you are given the topic, you can dive right in and begin writing your masterpiece.

When building anything, whether a house, a sculpture, or essay, the person creating it has a plan in mind. This plan is his or her template and helps create what he or she envisions.

Your template is your key to doing well on the analytical portion of the GMAT, and it should follow a specific format, as follows.

- The first paragraph should address the issue, while offering two differing points on it. It should end with your final analysis.
- The second paragraph will present your reason for your position on the matter.
- Your third paragraph will present the second reason for your position on the matter.
- The fourth paragraph will present your best reason for your position on the matter.

- The last paragraph is your conclusion and will tie together the points that support your position on the argument presented in the essay question.

Your template can take other formats, as shown below. Each will work just as well for your essay and will help you pass this portion with flying colors.

Template 1

- State both sides of issue, then state what side you support
- Support your side
- Provide more support
- Provide more support
- Conclusion

Template 2

- State your position
- Make arguments in favor of the position you oppose
- Challenge each of those arguments
- Conclusion

Template 3

- State the position you oppose
- Go against the first position
- Give support for your position
- Provide further support
- Conclusion

Now that you have organized your essay, you have to begin thinking about how to support your point of view. You can do this by quickly writing out your outline from the template and jotting down your supporting ideas in bullet point form. Then, go through the question again and pick out what you will use as your support or what you will use as your evidence against the argument in the question.

This will allow you to determine what points will be strong, what will not, and what you need to add.

The Second Topic

The second topic uses many of the same points that you learned from how to write for the first topic. There is, however, one major change. The analysis of argument essay must be approached like an argument in the critical reasoning section.

As a result, you should follow these steps to ensure that you do well here.

1. Read the entire essay.
2. Identify the essay's assumptions and think of other assumptions that you can use.
3. Identify the premise of the essay.
4. Determine the template that you will use.
5. Identify how the assumptions can be used to make a better argument.
6. Edit your essay when you have completed it.

In this topic, your graders will determine whether you identified and analyzed the important aspects of the argument, and whether you supported your main points and demonstrated a superior grasp of language, including the direction of your argument.

Your essay should typically conform to a single form, as follows.

- Summarize the conclusion of the argument in the first paragraph.
- In the second to fourth paragraphs, attack the argument and the evidence it uses to support itself.
- In the last paragraph, simply summarize what you have said and offer ways that the argument could be strengthened.

Tips and Tricks

Now that we have gone over how you should write the essay and attack the argument, what about the meat – the words that make up the essay?

You want to include certain words that will catch the eye of the reader and allow him or her to quickly skim through your essay. Readers only spend two minutes on essays, so you have only two minutes to impress them.

1. If you are making points in your essay, be sure to separate them and identify them using the words First, Second, Third, etc…
2. Whenever you support an argument with an example, which is important if you are trying to prove something, then you should use words like for example, to illustrate, for instance, and because.
3. If you are adding onto that example with additional support in the same paragraph, then use words like in addition, also, moreover, and furthermore.
4. If you want to emphasize the importance of something, then use the words surely, truly, clearly, certainly, in fact, and most importantly.
5. When you reach your conclusion, then use words such as therefore, hence, in conclusion, and in summary.

That's All Folks!

There you have it, the GMAT from top to bottom. Naturally, we can't cover absolutely everything you will see on the test. But now you have a much better understanding of the exam and are better prepared for it. It may seem like a lot of things are being tested, but when you get right down to it, you only need a handful of effective techniques and tools for the test. With the techniques and tools that you learned from this book, you can now enjoy success on the GMAT!

Made in the USA
Lexington, KY
07 December 2010